The Art of
LOUIS COMFORT
TIFFANY

The Art of
LOUIS COMFORT
TIFFANY

TESSA PAUL

Exeter Books

NEW YORK

FOR ZÖe

A QUINTET BOOK

First published in the USA 1987
by Exeter Books
Distributed by Bookthrift
Exeter is a trademark of Bookthrift Marketing, Inc.
Bookthrift is a registered trademark of
Bookthrift Marketing Inc., New York, New York.

ISBN 0 671 08889 0

This book was designed and produced by
Quintet Publishing Limited
6 Blundell Street
London N7 9BH

Art Director: Peter Bridgewater
Designer: Linda Moore
Editors: Patricia Bayer, Judith Simons
Illustrator: Lorraine Harrison

Typeset in Great Britain by
Central Southern Typesetters, Eastbourne
Manufactured in Hong Kong by
Regent Publishing Services Limited
Printed in Hong Kong by
Leefung-Asco Printers Limited

ACKNOWLEDGEMENTS

The author would like to thank Janet Zapata of Tiffany & Co,
New York for her help in forwarding reference material. Mr
Harold Jaffe of the Louis C Tiffany Society, Great Neck, New
York, who provided information. Mr Potter of the Haworth
Gallery, Accrington, Lancashire for his time and help. Many
thanks also to Mary Gray and Mary Linden-Kelly for typing the
manuscript, and to the author's family for their support and
encouragement.

CONTENTS

INTRODUCTION

Louis C Tiffany in his middle years.

●

RIGHT Nocturne in Black and Gold: The Falling Rocket *by James McNeill Whistler is an early expression of Art Nouveau.*

Louis Comfort Tiffany was a true child of the Art Nouveau era. His designs and his sense of beauty matched exactly the ideals of his time. Yet this observation should not carry the implication that he was a mere imitator of a fashionable artistic creed. On the contrary, Tiffany was one of the originals of Art Nouveau, and it was his work that set a standard for his peers.

A brief understanding of the ideas behind the Art Nouveau movement can be gained by looking at the work of James McNeill Whistler, whose techniques heralded the beginning of this style. His artistic ideas are outlined by Robert Schmutzler in *Art Nouveau.* In describing Whistler's painting *Nocturne in Black and Gold: The Falling Rocket,* Schmutzler says that the artist's 'fundamental attitude to his work is made clear: it is decorative, ornamental and musical. The picture is transformed into a sort of rhythmically formless ornament'.

The progenitors of Art Nouveau expressed this 'fundamental attitude' in images that refused to be representational, but instead concentrated the essence of flower, fish, bird and human forms, and transformed them into decorative symbols. They were much influenced, as was Whistler, by the flat, linear images of the Japanese, and by the use of 'colour to distinguish objects ... one from an other'.[1] These artists made a design from a lily, or an iris, and painted smooth areas of colour to distinguish petal from leaf. Colour was no longer applied in a painterly manner, with confused tonality; the intricate reality of a plant was ignored. Design, pattern and symbol became paramount. Art Nouveau transformed the simplicity of Japanese design into a 'swinging, swirling, throbbing, sprouting and blossoming ... sign of organic life'.[2]

The concepts that shaped the Art Nouveau movement are those that guided Tiffany's own creative approach, but his work was, of course, inspired by influences wider and more profound than purely contemporary trends. His genius was fed by deeper sources, rooted in his childhood, nurtured by his father and enriched by an early intimacy with superb craftsmen. But his childhood did have odd parallels with developments in the contemporary art world. It was as if everything conspired to create an artist who would excel in the milieu of Art Nouveau.

Louis Comfort Tiffany was born into a wealthy merchant family, but more than this, his was a family that traded in beautiful things. His father was Charles Lewis Tiffany, founder of the legendary New York store, Tiffany & Co. Charles Tiffany and his partner opened a modest stationery and fancy goods store at 259 Broadway. Their stock was described then as bric-à-brac, but

*LEFT A portrait of
Charles Lewis Tiffany by
William Henry Powell,
painted in 1840.*

by the time Louis was born in 1848, the store had
become a jewelry shop for millionaires.

The success of this enterprise was due, in large
measure, to Charles Tiffany. Customers first noticed
Tiffany & Young because the window displays were so
unusual. Chinese parasols, Japanese papier-mâché,
leatherwork, terracotta dishes and fans were lovingly
displayed by Mr Tiffany and it was this mute aesthetic
appeal that initially attracted customers in search of the
exotic and the beautiful.

Charles Lewis Tiffany was born in 1812 in Connecticut, where his father owned a textile mill and a general
store. His family were descendants of Squire Humphrey
Tiffany who settled in Massachusetts Bay Colony around
1660. Charles, by the age of 15, was manager of this
store. When he moved to New York in 1837, his father
lent him the capital to start a business with John Young,
a school friend.

As the business expanded, the partners went on
shopping trips to Europe, seeking out suppliers of
Bohemian glass and Dresden porcelain, French clocks
and cutlery. Charles Tiffany, whose great love was
jewellery, built up a collection of historic gems. John
Young was in France when the price of diamonds

LEFT Charles L Tiffany and his partner opened their first shop at 259 Broadway in September 1837. Tiffany & Young was to develop into Tiffany & Co, but they did not move from these modest premises until 1847.

FAR LEFT This print depicts General Sheridan leading his men in the Battle of Cedar Creek, 1864. Their swords, epaulets and other military paraphernalia were probably supplied by Tiffany & Co. The Civil War served, among other things, to build the vast personal fortune of Charles Lewis Tiffany, who turned his jewelry showrooms into a military supply store for the Unionist troops.

dropped by half during the 1848 revolutionary disturbances in Europe, and he was directed by Charles Tiffany to purchase a huge stock. Charles was keenly aware of the market upheavals on the Continent and turned it to his benefit. He bought diamonds from the fabulous collection of the Hungarian Prince Esterhazy. At the French Government sales, he bought 24 lots of diamonds, among them the zone of diamonds, which had belonged to Marie-Antoinette, and jewels from Louis XV.

Imagine the home in which this child, Louis C Tiffany, found himself. He was not surrounded by the plain, the ugly or even the simple. His senses were besieged – his hands pressed the curled and ridged handles of French silver cutlery; he spooned up his food, only to reveal the floral design of a Dresden plate; he held delicate porcelain to his lips; perhaps he and his sisters played with an old Chinese parasol and traced the birds and flowers painted on its waxy surface. These things must have delighted and impressed the boy, because as an adult he sought to repeat the aesthetic sensations of his childhood and it is perhaps significant that Tiffany was at his best when he worked at a small, detailed level of creativity.

If Louis inherited this love of the rare and beautiful from his father, his mother had a, perhaps, less artistic influence. Harriet was the sister of Charles' partner, John, and the daughter of Judge Ebenezer Young of Connecticut. Her principles were strictly Congregationalist, and she hoped to raise her children with a common-sense severity. Louis was her third son. She had lost her first boy in his fourth year, and her second son before he was a year old, so Louis must have been precious to her. But he was a wilful and dreamy child, proud, solitary and capricious. His two sisters, Annie and Louise, were of a milder temperament, and the youngest child, Burnett, was often victim to his older brother's teasing.

Louis' unpredictable nature disrupted family life, and defeated his mother's stern principles. He was sent to boarding school, Flushing Academy on Long Island, and then to a military academy.

How did this artistic boy respond to such an institution? Perhaps he pursued his old interests, strolling on the beach, collecting bits of glass worn smoothly dim by the relentless sea; seeking out curious pebbles and stones; perhaps his vision of war was coloured by his father's military activities and, if so, the boy may not

have noticed any army discipline, but observed instead military paraphernalia.

For Charles Tiffany, in his own way, was active in the Civil War. At the outbreak of hostilities, Mr Tiffany submitted a complete model of the equipment of the French Army to the Quartermaster General. His elegant showrooms were transformed into a depot for military supplies. Tiffany & Co advertised 'swords from Solingen Passants; cap ornaments . . . from Paris; gold epaulettes . . . from London'. The state of Ohio alone ordered 20,000 badges. Tiffanys supplied and manufactured swords, boots, caps, rifles, medals and badges, even ambulances, and Charles Tiffany became a wealthy man.

So it was not only an appreciation of the beautiful that Louis learnt from his father. He also discerned a sharp commercial sense behind the gorgeous clutter of *objets d'art.* Perhaps the 10-year-old boy watched when, in 1858, the police had to control crowds of souvenir hunters who besieged his father's store. Mr Tiffany had bought up the remainders of the first Great Atlantic Cable, and had cut them up into paperweights, umbrella handles, bracelets. New York shoppers rushed to buy these novelties. Louis C Tiffany's own commercial success later in life owed something, perhaps, to his childhood, which was, in all senses, that of a little mercantile prince.

But there was another influence in Louis' boyhood. This was the master silversmith who worked with Tiffany and Young. (The store became Tiffany & Co in 1853.) In 1848, Charles Tiffany had opened a workshop where he gathered together jewelry makers and silversmiths. His first master silversmith was John C Moore, who worked for Marquarand & Co, but agreed that Tiffany would be his sole client. He was followed by his son, Edward C Moore.

Edward C Moore was a remarkable craftsman, designer and art connoisseur, of whom Samuel Bing said 'his country should forever shrine him in grateful memory'.[3] In his superior role in the fashionable Tiffany workshops, Edward C Moore influenced many young artists and craftsmen in New York. By all accounts, he was generous with advice, and through his work and his intense interest in art, especially *objets d'art,* he introduced a new perspective to American sensibilities. Moore looked not to Europe for his inspiration, but to the East. He admired Islamic and Persian art, with their geometric abstractions of natural forms and sumptuous intricacy of design. Later, he became absorbed by Japanese art and its masterful use of metals. He invited a team of Japanese metal craftsmen to New York. Under their guidance, in the Tiffany & Co workshops, tonalities of every kind were mixed with silver, and experiments in enamel work conducted.

RIGHT Archaeological excavations in the 19th century brought to light the beauty of ancient glassware, such as this Roman vase of blown glass dating from the 2nd century AD. Tiffany, as a youth, studied such examples in Moore's collection and in the Victoria and Albert Museum, London.

In his own work as a silversmith, Moore developed a style that Bing defined as Saracenic. This style, though based on Japanese and Moorish designs, was strongly individual in its interpretation of these Oriental models. He was the first American to win a European award for his craft, and, under the auspices of Tiffany & Co, won the Gold Medal at the 1878 Paris Exposition. His interests were not confined to his own craft. He was a great collector of *objets*, and had a splendid collection of Oriental and antique glass.

This man was a familiar part of Louis' childhood. Moore had worked with, or for, Tiffany & Co since 1851. Louis grew up in the shadow of the Tiffany workshops, and, even as a child, was privy to the techniques and methods of craftsmen. Edward C Moore was a worldly, subtle man and he imbued the young boy with his knowledge and sophisticated enthusiasm. He encouraged Louis to study non-European art, and, as the boy grew older, persuaded him to collect objects of interest. Moore exposed Louis to Oriental art forms, and later, in his interior designs, Louis was to reveal his affinity with the opulence of Islamic design.

And – if the child is father to the man – Louis was entranced by Moore's glass collection. For glass proved to be the great passion in Tiffany's life, and although it was some years before he concentrated upon this passion, it was his work in glass that brought Tiffany recognition as a truly original artist.

●

LEFT His admiration
for ancient glass
inspired Tiffany to
devote himself to
years of
experimentation with
texture and technique.
This iridescent glass
vase, created around
1892, demonstrates
his passion for the
shape and colour of
Roman glass.

EAST WEST ENCOUNTERS

*Entrance to the prayer hall of the Qarawiyin Mosque at Fes,
Morocco. Islamic architecture delighted the young Tiffany as he
travelled around the Middle East, and it had a profound influence
on his style as an interior designer.*

Louis left school in 1866. Despite his mother's hopes, his formal education taught him to loathe authority. His was not a submissive, but a 'competitive nature ... non-conformist, individualistic, exacting and auto-cratic'.[1] He was a perfectionist, and he was self-confident. These traits, combined with great wealth, gave him formidable advantages.

Louis Comfort Tiffany started his adult life as a painter. There was no argument or discussion from his family when he announced his intention to be an artist. No doubt, his father had long since given up any hope that the boy would join him in business. After all, Louis had always been a wayward child, but Charles must have realized that the boy was creative and extremely energetic. Louis proved worthy of his father's trust. He did not scamper around town, acting the playboy on his father's money; he was a serious art student.

However, his approach to his studies had the stamp of eccentricity. He did not attend classes with fellow students, but roamed Manhattan, sketching endlessly. He often visited the studio of George Inness, an Ameri-can painter working in the style of the Barbizon School. This was the title given to the group of French painters who worked in the village of Barbizon near Fontaine-bleau. Its chief members were Millet, Théodore, Rousseau and Diaz, 'their aims being an exact and un-prettified rendering of peasant life and scenery, painted on the spot'.[2]

Inness was responsible for introducing these aims to the American art world and he was chief among a growing number of artists who, after the Civil War, looked towards a greater realism in their work. They, like their European counterparts, had responded to the visual impact of the camera. They painted, not with a careful description of objects as they knew them to be, but as they sensed them, with the landscape, the trees, the world, broken by light and shadow and movement.

Robert Koch, in his biography of Tiffany, says that Inness, 'impressed by the restless, intense, well-dressed young man gave him some small canvases and some paints to see what he could do, and Tiffany became his first and only pupil'.[3] Tiffany's output was prodigious and aroused 'both the respect and envy of his contem-poraries'.[4] And he was a fine painter. Within a year, in 1867, the National Academy of Design in New York exhibited his painting *Afternoon*.

Inness was inclined to entertain in his studio, and Tiffany met various young men from the cultural world of New York. The playwright, James Steele MacKaye, was chief among those who stimulated Louis' interest in the 'artistic life'. But Louis found that his restless and inquisitive nature needed further horizons and he

decided to visit Europe. He was a rich young American and he had an entrée to the artistic worlds of Paris and London through his father's business connections. In 1868, Charles Tiffany had opened branches of his store in Paris and London, and he had watchmaking factories in Geneva. But even now, Louis was not idle. He travelled as a student of art, and, as in New York, he sought individual tuition. Tiffany came to Europe when the Middle East was enjoying a certain vogue. Archaeologists were busy in Greece and Egypt and the Holy Land and European sensibilities were excited by the glamour of the Ottoman Empire, the North African desert and the culture of Islam.

There was a school of painting that concentrated on these Oriental scenes. Léon Bailly, along with Jean-Léon Gérôme and a host of others, painted in this genre. Tiffany, whose childhood had cultivated a taste for the exotic, and especially the exotic East, was naturally attracted to this school of painting and in the winter of 1868/1869 studied in Bailly's studio.

He did not stay long in Paris, but determined to travel and explore. While wandering through Spain – where he must have visited the Alhambra and thrilled to the Moorish architecture – he met another young American painter, Samuel Colman. According to Robert Koch, it was Samuel Colman who taught Tiffany the use of watercolour and gave him the habit of making sketches in this medium. It was a habit that was to last the rest of Louis' long life.

The two young painters travelled to North Africa together, landing initially in Oran. Colman was excited by Islamic textiles, Tiffany by architecture. Tiffany's skill at architectural drawing, his instinctive grasp of bulk and form, became apparent in his Islamic studies. His love of detail also began to manifest itself in these sketches – the latticework of an Islamic balcony, the patterned tiles on a wall were precisely reproduced in his work.

His father's money allowed the young painter full scope to travel and experiment. In 1870 Louis travelled to Gibraltar, to Egypt, to Venice and Italy, Tangiers and Bohemia. Everywhere he went, he sketched and observed – the Islamic buildings, their interiors, their lamps, their fittings; he studied Romanesque churches, their massive domes and arches; he stood entranced before the great stained glass windows of Europe's cathedrals.

Tiffany had a profound intellectual curiosity, but not for philosophies or theories. His was a creative energy; he wanted to understand the construction of things, of buildings, of lamps, of furniture, of glass, and how machines operated; he was intrigued by the effects of light and shade, by colours and shapes. These are the

CHAPTER ONE

•

LEFT Samuel Colman, the watercolourist, was a collector of textiles. He travelled with Tiffany in the Middle East and both artists were fascinated by the intricate designs they saw. Tiffany was to build a huge collection of Oriental carpets. This 16th-century needlework carpet is from Turkey and is now in the Topkapi Museum, Istanbul.

19

things he explored, and observed, and read about. His travels were, for him, journeys of artistic and technical discovery.

There is no evidence of the social world inhabited by Tiffany while he visited the Continent. Presumably, he called on Tiffany & Co when in London, and probably went to the 'Oriental Warehouse' run by Arthur Lasenby Liberty. This was an outlet for Japanese prints, drawings, lacquer, porcelain, and bronzes, and, as an enthusiastic collector, Tiffany would have shopped here. Also, he would have spent some time in the Victoria and Albert Museum (then called the South Kensington Museum), where there was a unique collection of antique Roman, Persian, and Venetian glass.

Mario Amaya writes in *Tiffany Glass* that 'it is not too far-fetched to assume that a rich young American in London – especially with social connections – and particularly one interested in art – would have met the small circle that included Morris, Rossetti, Burne-Jones, not to mention his compatriot, Whistler'. These men

were artists, given to intellectual ideals. They wrote, and talked, a great deal about the role of the artist in society. William Morris was their acknowledged leader and the high priest of the Arts and Crafts Movement. But Tiffany was not a man given to intellectual conversations. Koch tells us that 'he [Tiffany] was impatient with the limitations of language and found it impossible to explain or express himself without gestures and effects. Even in simple conversation he had considerable difficulty'.[5]

The ideas behind the Arts and Crafts Movement must have seemed, in 1869, very remote to the youthful Tiffany. He had grown up in the lavish and extrava-

LEFT Spectacular mosaic work can be found in mosques all over the Arab world. Tiffany was overwhelmed by interiors such as the Blue Mosque in Istanbul. Years later, he was to reproduce the same effect in his design for a chapel, which was exhibited at the 1983 World Fair in Chicago.

BELOW LEFT (INSET) Early in his travels, Tiffany visited Spain. He was excited by the decorative wall surfaces and the colours found in Moorish architecture, exemplified in the former Great Mosque in Cordova.

gant world of *nouveau-riche* New York, which grew and fattened on industrial advancement. Tiffany would have been bewildered by a Europe struggling to come to terms with industrialization and bored by the thinkers and intellectuals in England who were devising social systems to cope with life under the machine.

The Arts and Crafts Movement started as a romantic longing for medieval workshops, where artist and artisan worked as one in creative labour, beyond the stultification of mechanical production. There was a belief that, before technology, everyone had lived with simple, functional but beautiful hand-crafted furniture and household goods. The historic reasons, and the hopes, behind the Arts and Crafts Movement are described by C R Ashbee in *Where the Great City Stands*. He wrote that industrialization, and with it, 'The disappearance of small workshops with the guild system that regulated human labour and set its standard of quality in life and work in man's hands, is more far-reaching than any religious or dynastic change. But the Arts and Crafts Movement made the discovery that it was only in the small hand workshop that those things could be had again for which that movement stood'. The movement was a self-conscious attempt to deny industrialization and factory labour, and to revive the 'simple life'.

Tiffany grew up with artist-artisans working together. For him it was a familiar organization of labour; his father did not harbour nostalgia for the past, but simply put men and machines, craftsmen and designers to work together. Louis was to remain, throughout his life, a fervent believer in craftsmen working together under one roof, and though he would one day borrow other ideas from the Arts and Crafts Movement, he never decried the advantages of modern technology.

It is likely that Louis, with his interest in the decorative arts and his commercial background, read the manifesto issued by Morris when that gentleman opened his own firm, Morris, Marshall, Faulkner & Co, in 1861. This announced that 'The growth of the Decorative Arts in [England] ... has now reached a point at which it seems desirable that Artists of reputation should devote their time to it .... The Artists whose names appear above ... will be able to undertake any species of decoration, mural or otherwise, from pictures ... down to the smallest work susceptible of art beauty'.

That approach, the idea of a firm of artists creating a total environment of beauty, may have buried itself in the Tiffany head, but if so, he did not brood upon it. He was just 21, he had had an exhilarating trip through the Old World – but now he was going home to concentrate upon his painting.

A RICH USE OF PAINT

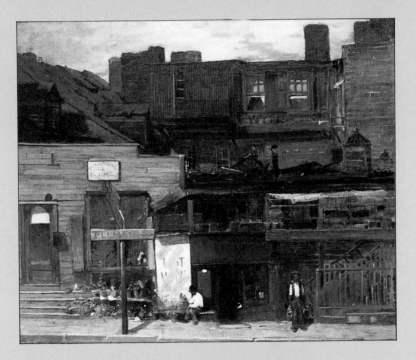

Duane Street, New York *painted by Louis C Tiffany in 1875,
alarmed his contemporaries with its squalid realism, and
presaged the 'Ashcan School' of the early 20th century.*

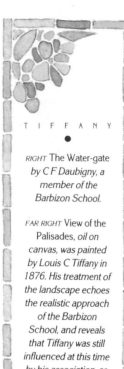

RIGHT The Water-gate by C F Daubigny, a member of the Barbizon School.

FAR RIGHT View of the Palisades, *oil on canvas, was painted by Louis C Tiffany in 1876. His treatment of the landscape echoes the realistic approach of the Barbizon School, and reveals that Tiffany was still influenced at this time by his association, as a young art student, with Georges Inness.*

On his return to New York, Louis C Tiffany elected not to live in his parents' home at 212 Fifth Avenue. He rented a studio at the YMCA, which was strategically placed across the road from the National Academy of Design on 23rd Street.

Years later, Tiffany was to berate his fellow Americans when he spoke of his feelings as a young artist. He told them 'I returned to New York wondering why we made so little use of our eyes, why we refrained so obstinately from taking advantage of colour in our architecture and our clothing'. He said, 'I had a chance to travel in the East and to paint where the people, and the buildings also, are clad in beautiful hues [so] . . . the pre-eminence of colour was brought forcibly to my attention'.

Tiffany's paintings are remarkable for their warmth and harmony of colour. He regarded line and form as of secondary importance. 'It is curious, is it not, that line and form disappear at a short distance, while colour remains visible at a much longer?' he observed once. 'It is fairly certain – isn't it? – that the eyes of children at first see only coloured surfaces . . . colour and movement, *not* form, are our earliest impressions'.

It was his instinctive understanding of colour, his bold delight in colour, that make his 'Oriental' genre paintings some of his most beautiful works. Gertrude Speenburgh in *The Art of the Tiffanys* lists four and claimed that these were important. They are *Mosque and Market Place, Ruins of Tangiers, Citadel of Cairo* and *View of the Nile*. These genre paintings were perfect vehicles for Tiffany's own obsessions with decoration and colour. *The Snake Charmer at Tangiers* depicts a group of people as they watch, what was for the occidental observer, a bizarre entertainment. Tiffany has reproduced the rich colours of the carpeted floor, the textures and hues of Arab clothing, the basketwork, the snake. He has placed the group in a courtyard, but they are overwhelmed by the brilliant light upon tall pillars, the deep shade of the interior behind, and the warm colours of roof tiles and high desert sky. In his study *Walkway in Tangiers* Tiffany painted an Arabic city where the 'amplitude of line at once picturesque and simple [is] . . . enhanced by colouring that . . . [is] sumptuous without being violent'[1] – words used by Bing in another context, but a perfect description of what Tiffany sought to achieve in all his work.

In New York, Tiffany began to use painting techniques closer to those of the Impressionists. He introduced this school to the American Watercolor Society, which had been founded by his friend, Samuel Colman. However, he continued his old habit of painting alfres-

co, often in Manhattan, in Connecticut, on the beach and in the hills. In *View of the Palisades* his appreciation of simple, massive shapes, enriched by colour and detail, is again apparent. His love of buildings and his skill as an architectural draughtsman are evident in many of his paintings at this time.

Tiffany may have been a romantic and a great lover of nature, yet he was hardly the bucolic sort. He never lived a rural life, although he owned country estates where his family spent their summers. He looked to nature for colour and inspiration rather than as a subject to be painted. As the Chinese and the Japanese 'derived their colours and textures from such things in nature as butterfly wings, skins of animals and reptiles, plumage of birds and markings of shells,[2] so Tiffany regarded nature. He said of flowers 'that their form is distinctly a secondary consideration which comes after the satisfaction we feel in their colour'.

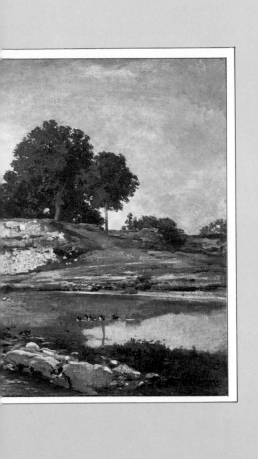

It was in his urban studies that Louis Tiffany showed his originality. His painting of a city slum, *Duane Street, New York* was highly praised. I H Baur in *Revolution and Tradition in Modern American Art* claimed that this painting 'marked the beginning of a new approach to the urban landscape'. Tiffany was only 27 when he painted *Duane Street*, yet he anticipated, 30 years in advance, the American Ashcan School, who were to exhibit their paintings in New York in 1908. The aim of this school was 'to found an American art based on a realistic portrayal of the contemporary scene'.[3]

Tiffany the painter has been rather neglected since his death, but he was recognized and highly regarded in the artistic circles of his time. He exhibited at the Philadelphia Centennial of 1876 and at the 1878 Paris Exposition. The National Academy of Design in New York displayed his work, as did the Century Club. He rarely sold his paintings, and, perhaps, this fact has

facilitated their neglect. For many years, they were in family and private collections, and very few museums were able to exhibit them.

Tiffany combined real organizational ability with creative talents, and used these to great effect. He was active in promoting and supporting the work of other artists. In 1870, he was elected to the Century Club, and in 1871 became an Associate Member of the National Academy of Design. He was a member of the American Watercolor Society, of which Samuel Colman was President, and he helped found the Society of American Artists, of which he was Treasurer. There were other artists with studios in the YMCA, men such as Swain Gifford, William Sartain and Edwin Austin Abbey. The Society of American Artists included George Inness and John La Farge. All these men knew each other, and occasionally even worked together, but among them, Colman was Tiffany's closest friend. Although Colman was a watercolourist, his real interest was in textiles, and because of this, he was to be directly responsible for moving Tiffany away from painting and into the field of applied art.

Other factors conspired to distract Tiffany from his painting. His own creative force drove him to seek other forms of expression. He had started experiments in glass in 1875 on the basis that his talents need not be confined to one medium. His old mentor, Edward C Moore, encouraged this line of thought. Moore liked things, objects; he was interested in their construction, their shape and design, and he knew that Tiffany not only shared his enthusiasm, but also had the technological skill and ability to be an artist-craftsman.

Tiffany was also exposed to enthusiasm for the

●

LEFT On the way between Old and New Cairo, Citadel Mosque of Mohammed Ali, and Tombs of the Mamelukes, *oil on canvas, was painted by Louis Comfort Tiffany c 1872. The scene is based on his travels in North Africa.*

applied arts through members of his family. His sister, Annie, married Alfred Mitchell in 1871, whose brother, Donald G Mitchell, was a keen admirer of the French architect Viollet-le-Duc, the great restorer of ancient buildings in France and expert in stained-glass windows. Donald Mitchell, himself, was to be a judge of applied arts at the Philadelphia Centennial in 1876, and designed the Connecticut Building for this exhibition. He also had literary interests and wrote essays under the name of Ike Marvel.

The two men had much in common, and their friendship had a sentimental bond, too, for it was in Mitchell's home that Louis met Mary Woodbridge Goddard. He married her in New York on 15 May 1872. Mary thought Louis was a genius, and, presumably, was happy for him to bring his fellow artist, Samuel Colman, along on a family trip to Brittany in the summer of 1874. Their first child was a year old when they took this painting holiday, but Mary lost her second baby in that year. She also contracted tuberculosis, and her health was permanently impaired.

On their return to New York, the Tiffanys lived at 48 East 26th Street, but spent much time at Charles Tiffany's country home in Irvington-on-Hudson. Louis painted numerous charming studies of his family at this time, and became interested in the camera as yet another medium of creative expression. Gertrude Speenburgh claims that Louis Comfort Tiffany 'experimented in phases of photography and was the first to take instantaneous pictures of birds and animals'.[4]

Back in New York, Tiffany must have been aware of new ideas stirring in the world of architecture and household designs. Donald Mitchell would talk about design, and of English craftsmen and illustrators. Samuel Colman and Edward Moore were absorbed by similar interests. They would all be excited by the exhibitions at the Philadelphia Centennial.

ABOVE LEFT *Peacocks, often used as a motif by Art Nouveau designers, were embroidered on this screen exhibited by the Royal School of Art Needlework.*

ABOVE RIGHT *Candace Wheeler, portrayed here in this marble bas-relief by L Thompson, was an enthusiastic force in the American revival of embroidery as an art form.*

ABOVE FAR RIGHT *The Horticultural Hall at the Centennial revealed a growing Oriental influence on design.*

1876 PHILADELPHIA CENTENNIAL

The 1876 Philadelphia Centennial was staged to celebrate one hundred years of independence, and to exhibit the nation's progress in trade, manufacture and the decorative arts. It also promoted cultural exchange between the United States and Europe.

American designers were stimulated by the English exhibits, which included wallpaper designed by the illustrator Walter Crane, and a beautiful screen of embroidered peacocks from the Royal School of Art Needlework. Samuel Colman and a fellow collector of textiles, Candace Wheeler, were particularly impressed by this screen. Mrs Wheeler was herself a master of embroidery, but her interests extended to all forms of design. She had followed the work of William Morris, and was grateful for the attention he had given to needlecraft. Mrs Wheeler felt that 'the designs of William Morris, Burne-Jones ... and the graceful work of Walter Crane, founded upon forms of growth ... skillfully adapted to needlework, gave great value to the new revival of embroidery'.[5]

Many exhibits at the Centennial hinted at a revival in the applied arts. Americans observed that the English were working towards a closer union between artist and craftsman. The English were, of course, inspired by a moral revulsion against industrialization and were looking for a return to the age of craft. But the Americans admired rather than deplored the power of industry, and were at some loss as to how to marry their craft to their factories.

Candace Wheeler preferred the English attitude to craft. She not only admired the work of the Royal School of Art Needlework but was sympathetic with its stated aim to promote profitable handicraft among women. She determined that the women of New York would earn money from their skills, and helped found the Society of Decorative Art 'to encourage profitable industries among women' and 'to establish rooms for exhibition and sale'. Samuel Colman gave Mrs Wheeler his full support, and helped her to start classes in which women would be taught art needlecraft, pottery and tile-painting.

Louis Tiffany exhibited his Oriental genre paintings at the Centennial and Tiffany & Co won a special gold award for their metalware. Louis paid close attention to the stained glass work on display, and was encouraged by the promotion this craft was given by Donald Mitchell who, as chairman of the judges for the decorative arts, reported that coloured glass was 'full of suggestion to those living in cities whose rear windows look upon neglected or dingy areas or courts, where the equipment of a window with rich designs would be a perpetual delight'.

CHAPTER THREE
FASHIONABLE MAGNIFICENCE

*A Japanese swordguard made from an alloy of copper and silver.
Louis C Tiffany had an enormous collection of these and used
Japanese design as source material for his own work.*

Louis C Tiffany chose fine art as a career, but his wealth allowed him to pursue other interests. In 1875, he had started glass experiments in the Thill glasshouse in Brooklyn. He travelled widely, and collected antique Greek and Roman glass. He also collected Oriental domestic ware. There was little of Europe in his choice and nothing that would have been recognized as 'art' in the classical sense.

Tiffany was absorbed by what he called 'the quest for beauty' and it intrigued him to find this quest answered even in the most humble household item. He said, 'Art interprets the beauty of ideas and visible things, making them concrete and lasting. When the savage searches [for] the gems from the earth or the pearls from the sea to decorate his person, or when he decorates the utensils of war and peace in designs and colours, he becomes an artist . . . he has turned his face to the quest for beauty'.

The utensils Louis sought and collected represented good craftsmanship or illustrated special working techniques. Often they carried designs drawn from nature. They were all both functional and decorative and they included enamelled boxes and tea jars from Japan, an enormous selection of Japanese *inro* and swordguards (which he purchased after the Emperor Meiji's Reforms in 1868 had directed the Japanese army to carry firearms rather than swords), Chinese jade bowls, embroidered screens and temple carpets, ivory jewellery, tortoiseshell combs, porcelain pots and jugs, medieval Persian rugs, Egyptian beads, Islamic wall tiles and textiles.

LEFT *Glass tiles and stained glass were incorporated in the interior designed by Louis C Tiffany and Associated Artists for Dr William T Lusk's dining room in 1882. The drapes and carpet reveal Colman's interest in ornate textiles.*

Tiffany studied everything he collected and grew familiar with the techniques of pottery, enamelling and tiling. But essentially he surrounded himself with these things because of their beauty. He had a profound belief that beauty could not be learned as much as absorbed. He never trusted learning as much as he did this process of 'osmosis', and was convinced that access to nature and lovely surroundings would nurture an understanding of beauty in any human soul. Nevertheless, when his old friend Samuel Colman approached him to teach the women at the Society of Decorative Art, Louis was pleased to help. With another connoisseur and collector, Lockwood de Forest, Louis gave lessons in making unbaked pottery.

Louis C Tiffany found no satisfaction in this gentle, amateur approach and he was not given to discussion, much less *chatter* about 'art'. The craft and design interested him, but the limitations of the classes aroused his impatience. He told Mrs Wheeler in the spring of 1879, 'You can't educate people without educational machinery, and there is so much discussion about things of which, really, there is no question'. But he acknowledged her creative direction and added, 'I have been thinking a great deal about decorative work, and I am going into it as a profession. I believe there is more in it than painting pictures'.

Tiffany could not have timed his decision at a more apt moment. America was in a period of industrial boom. Architects and engineers were developing new materials and working methods, calculating new economies of scale and conceiving new forms of building. Architects were creating a fresh vernacular, its earliest expression being in the work of H H Richardson, with his 'Romanesque' themes, and in the Shingle style, which had a massive austerity. The great capitalist entrepreneurs were commissioning lavish buildings for their homes and their businesses. They needed furnishings, fittings, and lighting devices.

LOUIS C TIFFANY AND ASSOCIATED ARTISTS

Louis C Tiffany sensed the opportunity to demonstrate his own ideas on the intermarriage of architecture and design. He perceived that the talents struggling for expression, at that time, in the Society of Decorative Art could be given greater scope through a proper level of professionalism and he invited Candace Wheeler, Samuel Colman and Lockwood de Forest to join him in a design venture. Behind this apparent commercial opportunism, there was an intense private dream. As a very young man travelling in the Levant he had been impressed by Byzantine basilicas and their dazzling mosaics, which created glittering effects through their combination of glass and colour. Tiffany longed to create rooms glowing with rich colour, yet subtly lit through tinted glass. He hated the prevailing timidity of dim interiors and traditional European style.

The group operated under the name Louis C Tiffany and Associated Artists, and Louis negotiated with the Society of Decorative Art for exclusive rights to design, supervise and sell the work of its members. One of the earliest commissions the group was given was the design of the drop curtain at the Madison Square Theater. The new theatre was to open in February 1880 with *Hazel Kirke*, written by Tiffany's friend from his student days, James Steele MacKaye. 'Instead of calling in upholsterers with conventional notions' reported one newspaper, 'Mr MacKaye secured the aid of Louis C Tiffany, one of the foremost of young painters and a noted colorist; as a result we

have a revelation of beauty'. Tiffany was responsible for the design and various ingenious innovations. Colman and de Forest were the colour and textile consultants, and Wheeler supervised the work. Mrs Wheeler, with her admiration for the tender embroideries of William Morris and Walter Crane, must have been startled by Tiffany's approach to her particular craft. Where Morris concentrated on lovely flowing

patterns using conventional threadwork to trace his designs, Tiffany made free use of paint, thread and fabrics, thus creating a collage of textiles and stitches.

The drop curtain was an experiment in new methods of appliqué, in design and colour, and in materials. The whole was embroidered and painted on a background of velvet and satin. Unfortunately the curtain was destroyed by fire but it was replaced with a replica.

ABOVE Candace Wheeler and her team translated Tiffany's design for the drop curtain at the Madison Square Theater. His fresh approach to the old craft of embroidery was typical of the man's unconventional ideas on design.

34

While Candace Wheeler and her seamstresses had been working on the drop curtain, Tiffany and Colman had been designing wallpapers for the New York firm of Warren, Fuller & Co. Louis also continued his work in glass, and in 1878 established a glass-making house of his own. He travelled that year with his old mentor, Edward Moore, to the Paris Exposition, where the silversmith won a Gold Medal, and his father, Charles Tiffany, was created a Chevalier de la Légion d'Honneur. They met Samuel Bing, the dealer in Oriental artefacts, who in 1895 would open his famous 'Maison de l'Art Nouveau'. It was the start of a long friendship, particularly auspicious for Louis, as Bing was later instrumental in introducing Tiffany's glass work to Europe.

George Kemp, a pharmaceutical merchant who lived on Fifth Avenue and a friend of Charles Tiffany, asked Louis C Tiffany and Associated Artists to decorate his home. Louis was the designer and his taste for a rich Oriental theme, embellished with warm colour and ornate detail, decided the decor. Samuel Colman supplied the ornaments, wood carvings came from Lockwood de Forest's collection, and Candace Wheeler supervised the hangings. The ceiling of the salon had an Islamic-style interlace from which exotic lamps were hung. The walls were covered with flat decorative patterns, each framed individually, and Tiffany lined the fireplace with his own glass tiles. In the dining room, Tiffany placed panels of opalescent glass in the transoms above the doors. One panel was of gourds, the other of eggplants. More significantly, Tiffany took the glass left over from this work and created for his own studio a window that was totally abstract in design.

Louis C Tiffany's dream of the perfect interior was always interrupted by the demands of the client and he appeared to many, more interested, in his glass experiments than in the work of Associated Artists. *Scribner's Monthly* of July 1881 recorded that 'Mr Tiffany [should be] convinced that the planning of a work of monumental dignity demands more of him ... than the preparation of a single sketch and the selection of specialists to advise as to the details as well as to execute them'. But Tiffany's was a quick, vigorous talent that conceived the grand design, and knew how to employ the skills of others to realize it. His master hand remained obvious in all of Associated Artists' undertakings. Their interiors had an exotic Islamic air, and Tiffany's predilection for opulent colour and intricate design dominated their style. Under his direction, the group became extremely fashionable. The women of the Society of Decorative Art, as well as numerous anonymous craftsmen, were profitably employed through his workshop.

Among the many commissions they undertook were the private homes of Cornelius Vanderbilt II, of the Metropolitan Museum's founder J Taylor Johnston, of the Goelets, and of Mark Twain. They decorated the Union League Club, and won the commission to decorate the White House in Washington, DC.

One of the earliest public buildings the Associated Artists worked on was the Knickerbocker Greys' Seventh Regiment Armory on Park Avenue at 67th Street, where they were asked to design the Veterans' Room and Library. The architect was Charles W Clinton but Tiffany brought in Stanford White, then a pupil with H H Richardson, as his own consultant. Candace Wheeler, as always, was put in charge of the hangings.

Louis C Tiffany used Celtic and Japanese patterns in the high wooden wainscoting. Over the mantel, he placed a plaque of stucco and glass that showed a dragon and an eagle in battle. Glass tiles surrounded the large fireplace. The scheme was intended to symbolize the 'War Veteran' and the predominant materials were iron, leather and wood. Brocade hangings carried velvet motifs representing knighthood. Glass mosaics were suspended in front of the windows, filtering a golden light that softened the iron and wood. The Veterans' Room and Library were an immediate success, and brought Louis C Tiffany and Associated Artists general recognition as the most desirable decorators in New York.

Tiffany closed his own glasshouse – which had burnt down twice – and began experimenting at the Heidt glasshouse in Brooklyn. John La Farge was also conducting his glass experiments at Heidt's. Tiffany applied for a patent for a new character of glass in coloured windows. The glass tiles and lighting fixtures in many of

CHAPTER THREE
•

BELOW A prestigious commission at the start of their venture helped promote Associated Artists. This was the design for the Veterans' Room and Library in the Knickerbocker Grey's Seventh Regiment Armory. Symbolic use was made of iron and wood in these interiors, and the work was critically acclaimed.

●

LEFT Samuel Clemens, otherwise known as the author Mark Twain, commissioned Louis C Tiffany and Associated Artists to decorate his home in Hartford, Connecticut. His drawing room was allowed an elegant simplicity, free of the more extravagant touches so favoured by the design group.

RIGHT *Louis C Tiffany used his glass work as often as he could in his interior designs. Glass tiles and a stained-glass window dominate the dining room in Mark Twain's home.*

OPPOSITE ABOVE *With great skill and superb craftsmanship, Tiffany created an enormous glass screen for the White House. Despite a patriotic design of eagles and flags, it was to prove unpopular with later presidents.*

the interiors he had designed had already brought Tiffany considerable attention. *Scribner's Monthly*, in 1881, devoted an article to techniques in glass, mentioning Louis C Tiffany and John La Farge as leading exponents of the craft in America.

Associated Artists had by this time been commissioned to decorate the Vanderbilt home and the White House. In 1882 Louis left Candace Wheeler to cope with the petulant demands of Mrs Vanderbilt, while he concentrated his own efforts on the Washington commission. Chester Alan Arthur was in residence at the White House, or, rather, he was supposed to have moved in after the assassination of President James Garfield. However, Arthur refused to live in the White House, crying that the place looked like a badly-kept barracks. Associated Artists were asked to redecorate the corridor, the East Room, the Dining Room and the Red and Blue Parlors.

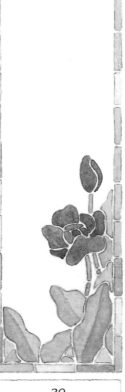

BELOW *Mr W S Kimball's library in Rochester, New York. Tiffany designed a wide arc to embrace the fireplace and windows. It acted also as a focus for the tiled chimney piece.*

In the Blue Parlor, Tiffany constructed four glass-mosaic sconces – 'each having seven gas-jets . . . each sconce provided with a background . . . three feet in diameter, composed of fantastic shapes of coloured glass interspersed with little mirrors . . . enhanced by the pendant drops of iridescent glass affixed to the arms that hold the jets'. The East Room – 'the largest parlor in the United States' – was given richly decorated beams in its high ceiling from which hung enormous chandeliers, each one made up of 6,000 pieces of Bohemian glass. Eight massive mirrors were set into the walls of the vast room, and the furnishings were in old gold. Louis C. Tiffany and Associated Artists supplied every detail from wall hangings and lights to shades and vases. The bill was for little more than $30,000 and the work was completed in a miraculous seven weeks. But Tiffany was straining the resources and patience of his colleagues. Mrs Wheeler wrote frantic letters to him in Washington about the Vanderbilt decorations. She complained that Mrs Vanderbilt refused to have certain-coloured drapes, and stated that she [Wheeler] was worried about the cost of the enterprise and the speed at which it had to be completed. De Forest made long trips to the Far East, and Colman had gone off to Newport.

Tiffany was lavish in his design, and his *pièce de résistance* was an opalescent glass screen that reached from the floor to the ceiling, and which featured an interlaced motif of eagles and flags. This screen separated the hallway between the East Room and the State Dining Room from the outer vestibule. When President Theodore Roosevelt moved into the White House in 1902, he instructed his architect Charles F McKim to demolish it.

BELLA
APARTMENT

Louis took more care in the decoration of his own home in New York, Bella Apartment, than in those places where the clients' whims were paramount. Here, his innovative spirit was allowed expression; he could fix abstract designs, and build fittings too original and, probably, too functional for his clients. All over the Bella Apartment there were signs of the originality and genius that Tiffany carried within him.

Yet these early years of the 1880s were sad and troubled times for Louis. In 1883, he parted from Associated Artists. Mary Tiffany had been treated for tuberculosis as early as 1874, and had received medical attention ever since. Her husband valued her companionship, for he was uneasy in company (he once wrote to Gustav Mahler that he was 'afraid of people'). That same year, 1883, Louis and Mary went to Florida in the hope that the warmer climate would restore her health, but to no avail. Mary died in New York the following year.

Designing interiors for clients was frustrating, but Tiffany found free expression in the family home, Bella Apartment, where he created a baronial air through the use of metal, firearms and tall, angular arches.

ABOVE The hallway featured an abstract stained-glass window. BELOW Over the mantle in the dining room, he hung an early American folk painting of a turkey and pumpkins. His use of decorative surfaces was wide and varied.

Louis fell into an emotional – and financial – mess. After parting from the Associated Artists, his section of the group became Louis C Tiffany and Co and was to retain the decorating aspects of the business. Candace Wheeler took the Associated Artists title. She had become a designer in her own right, and was creating wallpapers and textiles for manufacturing companies. Louis turned to theatre and music, his favourite distractions, but now he needed them for solace more than pleasure. Stanford White and James Steele MacKaye took him out and about to the nightspots of Broadway,

much to Charles Tiffany's quiet disapproval.

Stanford White at this time was occupied as architect for the new Lyceum Theater, and Tiffany was commissioned to decorate the auditorium. Louis had won this commission over John La Farge by the simple expedient of offering to do the work, not for a fee, but a percentage of the profits. The auditorium was a challenge to any designer, for it was the first to be completely lighted by electricity. Tiffany detested the pseudorichness that prevailed as a fashion for theatrical interiors, the lush, dark upholstery that absorbed and deadened light. He preferred to enhance the union of colour and light. He created an interior of a pale luminosity, the electricity gleaming through green sconces. Metropolitan theatregoers enjoyed for the first time a bright attractive auditorium, a far cry from the prevailing pompous 'velvet finish' (which still survives in some places today).

The new play was received less well than the new auditorium. *Dakolar,* written by MacKaye, closed after two months. The Lyceum was a financial disaster. The American Theater Building and Management Company, run by MacKaye and Gustave Frohman, could not pay Tiffany even to meet the cost of materials. Tiffany was forced to sue, and ended up owning the theatre. Frohman acted as manager and years later bought the theatre back from Tiffany, before it was demolished in 1902. Louis lost most of the money he had made with Associated Artists.

Charles Tiffany rescued his son from the unhappy mess that followed so soon after Mary's death. Charles wanted all his family under one roof, and he asked Louis to design and decorate the new home he had bought on 72nd Street at Madison Avenue. Louis Tiffany came close to realizing his youthful dream of a glorious harmony of light, colour, function and beauty in this building. He sketched the plan of a Romanesque apartment-mansion; McKim, Mead and White attended to the details. The mansion was subdivided to accommodate the different members of the Tiffany clan, and Louis designed the most lavish suite of all for himself. This suite was a studio and penthouse apartment. The main room had a chimney piece with four fireplaces and its smooth curvilinear forms make it the first example of plastically conceived American Art Nouveau. The extraordinary chimney piece was Tiffany's solution to an engineering problem. The design of the mansion dictated that all the chimney flues share an exit through the roof. Tiffany made the stack to which all the flues converged one of the chief decorative features of his suite and likened it to 'the bole of a great tree'.

Charles Tiffany had commissioned this huge apartment block for his sons and daughters to live in, but for some odd reason, refused to live there himself. Perhaps it was enough that the task of its construction served to divert Louis from what his father considered to be the decadent theatrical world. Charles was further pleased when Louis remarried in 1886, giving a mother to his three small children and himself a settled domestic life. Louise Wakeford Knox was the daughter of a Presbyterian minister and the Congregationalist faction in the Tiffany family approved his choice.

Louis Comfort Tiffany was now 38 years old. His early years had been marked by talent, enthusiasm,

energy, and experimentation, relatively careless of prevailing trends. But the Lyceum Theater experience had chastened him. Whereas previously he had scorned business, deliberately not following in his father's path, he now turned to his father as a model of professionalism, and with Charles' help reorganized his working life. Louis C Tiffany and Co began to work with and for architects and builders. The heady days of Associated Artists, young men and women decorating the homes of the rich, were past. Only occasionally in the future was Tiffany to take on a private commission. His workshops employed specialists and craftsmen, working in unison with other professional designers. Louis no longer tried to fill the roles of designer, glass maker, painter and salesman. He was the creative director, and he was the master designer, but he assumed the roles with a new maturity and authority. And he concentrated on his glass work.

LEFT The architecture and interior design for the new family home on 72nd Street at Madison Avenue were controlled by Louis C Tiffany. In his own suite, he built a soaring chimney piece and filled the air with hanging lamps, wrought-iron decorations and a suspended ostrich egg. The whole effect was lavish and extravagant.

THE MEDIEVAL MODEL

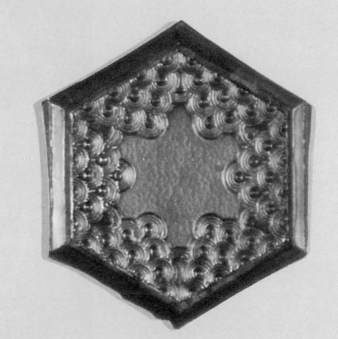

Louis C Tiffany's initial experiments in glass making
concentrated on the production of glass tiles, which he used
abundantly in his interior designs.

RIGHT In England, William Morris & Co was producing high-quality stained glass. British artists were not as pedantic as Tiffany and did sometimes use paint on their glass. These windows, in St Michael's Church, Brighton, Sussex, demonstrate how Morris incorporated the lead strips, or cames, into his stained-glass design.

Even as a child, Louis had a passion for glass, which ran parallel to his highly evolved sense of colour. Fortunately, he was not born in the 18th century, which branded glass work as an inferior craft. In his own time, glass work was enjoying a renewed status, the result of the English revival of the Gothic style. In America, great quantities of glass were being imported from England and Bavaria to decorate churches and secular buildings. William Morris and Burne-Jones were creating graphically designed stained-glass windows of velvet luminosity, but the material that came into the United States was not of such high quality. In fact, the Bavarian or 'Munich' glass was distinctly inferior.

Tiffany longed to reproduce the quality and techniques of medieval stained-glass work. He had visited cathedrals all over Europe to study the wonderful effects of stained glass. The jewel-like brilliance of medieval windows was the work of craftsmen who knew how to make richly coloured glass, and who developed techniques using the glass itself to express shading, clothing and facial details.

After the Reformation, the Protestant churches were decidedly less ornate than the great Catholic medieval cathedrals. A new humanism arose. The glass worker's skill was lost. Painters usurped the craftsmen's roles and began to work designs straight on to the glass. The craft degenerated into a mere imitation of painting.

Tiffany wanted no part of this degenerate method, believing that painted glass was both dull and artificial: 'I could not make an imposing window with paint.' He was not alone in this attitude. Two major analytical studies of medieval stained-glass techniques had been published in the 19th century. Viollet-le-Duc wrote of the methods he had learnt while restoring Chartres, and an Englishman, Charles Winston, published *Ancient Glass* in 1847. This volume had also greatly influenced Morris, Burne-Jones, Rossetti and Madox Brown in England. Winston was severe in his condemnation of brushwork on stained glass.

Medieval craftsmen cut glass pieces of various colours so that, when they were placed together, they formed the picture. Any shading or details were marked on the pieces with a solution of metallic oxides, which were fired into the glass. The pieces of glass were then held together with strips of lead. Winston called this the 'mosaic system of glass painting'. He pointed out that the lead strips, vital in the construction of the window, were an integral part of the design. If they were taken into consideration, he argued, very little shading or painting should be necessary.

William Morris translated this mosaic system into designs of large areas of pure colour, supported by a

Fear not ye, for I know that ye seek Jesus which was cr॥

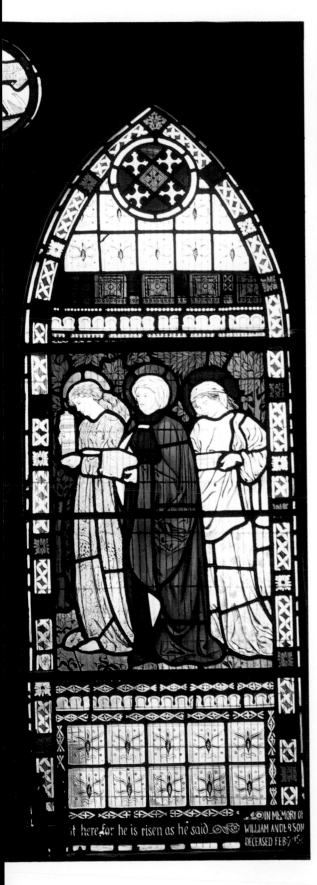

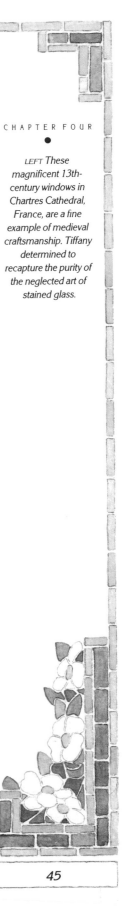

LEFT These magnificent 13th-century windows in Chartres Cathedral, France, are a fine example of medieval craftsmanship. Tiffany determined to recapture the purity of the neglected art of stained glass.

fretwork of lead strips. His central figures stand boldly against backgrounds of intricately leaded leaves and fruits, creating marvellous colour and balance between smaller and larger patterns. Louis C Tiffany, however, wanted the glass to express tonality and texture. He wanted to advance beyond the medieval method of marking the glass with metallic oxides, and find a way of creating depth with the colouring of the glass.

Louis C Tiffany was to become the most popular designer of stained glass in America. His designs and methods were copied by numerous other glass-workers. As a result, it is often difficult to identify a genuine Tiffany window, although some of his work for public buildings carried his markings. Both he and John La Farge experimented endlessly, producing quantities of opalescent glass, 'bull's-eye' glass and other original effects in colour and texture. As young men, these two artists were friends – both were founding members of the Society of American Artists – but they were to become bitterly competitive. It is uncertain which of them was the originator or innovator of the glass being produced in the Heidt glasshouse where they both worked.

Scribner's Monthly in 1881 noted that La Farge and Tiffany between them had virtually introduced a new glass industry and described part of the process. 'The hot glass, while at a red heat, is rolled with corrugated rollers, punched and pressed by various roughened tools, or is squeezed and pressed up into corrugations by lateral pressure, or it is stamped by dies. The "bulls-eyes" produced in making sheet glass, by whirling it round on a rod while still soft, are also cut into various shapes or ... are gently pressed into new shapes .... New styles of opalescent glass, new methods of mixing colors in the glasshouse, have also been tried, and with many surprising and beautiful results. Lastly comes one of the most original features of all, and this is the use of solid masses and lumps of glass, pressed while hot into the moulds, giving a great number of facets like a cut stone, or by taking blocks of glass and roughly chipping them into numerous small facets. These, when set in the window, have all the effects of the most brilliant gems, changing their shade of color with every changing angle of vision.'

Tiffany's technical virtuosity is compelling. The stippling of a bird's feather, the roughness of bark, the gleam of water, all are reproduced in the great pictorial windows he created, but none of these textures is drawn or marked into the glass. He used the mosaic system of the medieval craftsman, but his pieces of glass were not pure colour. They were a collage of colours, colours striped, mottled, patterned and spotted; the colour variations were themselves in the glass. He would match all the pieces into the design so that colours and textures flowed in a painterly manner. The absence of brushwork allowed the light to pass unhindered through the glass.

Louis Comfort Tiffany worked ceaselessly towards this aim of creating paintings in glass and it is in his abstract designs that he proved a master in stained glass. Before 1900, he designed stained-glass windows that made perfect use of glass as an artistic medium. In his abstract work, in which a geometry of coloured glass is delineated by the black line of the lead, Tiffany conveyed perfectly the use of light and design that made glass its own medium, no longer an imitation of painting. These abstracts were the logical demonstration of Charles Winston's theory that the lead strips have an integral design function in defining shape and separating colour in the mosaic system of stained glass. Even when the designs were not purely abstract, they showed the same natural flair for the medium of glass. Colour was flattened out into decorative shapes and emphasized with black outline. Tiffany, working in New York, baffled and intrigued by medieval glass design and technique, realized a cohesive unity of subject, material and picture plane similar to that achieved by the Nabis in Paris.

The Nabis were a small group of French painters who reacted against naturalism and whose belief in pure, flat colour is characterized by the famous instruction from one of the group, Maurice Denis: 'Remember that a picture, before being a horse, a nude or some kind of anecdote, is essentially a flat surface covered with colours assembled in a certain order.' A statement not so different from Tiffany's own observation that 'form ... is distinctly a secondary consideration, which comes after ... colour'.

It was his pictorial work, however, that made Louis Comfort Tiffany so fashionable in his own time. His stained-glass windows were commissioned by many architects, among them Charles C Haight, J C Cody and Robert H Robertson. These ornamental stained-glass windows could be seen in half the states of America, and in such illustrious institutions as the Smithsonian and Yale University, as well as private homes, hotels, libraries, churches bars and cafeterias too numerous to mention.

LEFT In 1890, Samuel Bing exhibited Tiffany's masterly stained-glass window, The Four Seasons, *in Paris, where it received great acclaim. The flat, decorative use of colour, with the plant forms reduced to their basic shapes and the whole surrounded by a lineal border of pure pattern, make this work an important example of early Art Nouveau. The panel pictured here represents 'Summer'.*

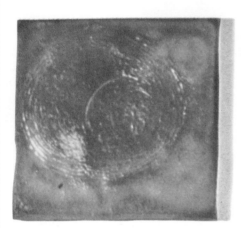  

GLASS TILES

Towards the end of the 1880s, Louis C Tiffany began to design a great deal of mosaic work. These glass tiles were the results of his early experiments in opalescent and iridescent glass. When he made his patent applications in 1880, he had specified three types of glass: one for use in tiles and mosaics, another for plating windows and a third to give a metallic lustre. This metallic lustre developed into his famous Favrile glass. It is important to recall that Tiffany did not invent the iridescent metallic lustre. When the Grosvenor Galleries opened in London they advertised 'bronze glass', borrowed from Dr Heinrich Schliemann's finds in Troy and Mycenae. In 1873, Ludwig Lobmeyr was selling iridescent glass products, and in England Thomas Webb and Sons produced iridescent glass in 1878. Tiffany never pretended to invent it, but he believed that he made the best iridescent glass. In his 1880 patent application, he conceded that it could also be produced by cor-roding the surface of the glass, such processes being well known to glass manufacturers.

When he conducted his early experiments, he achieved accidental effects that were quite beautiful. A spiral of colour would appear in marble glass, or a curious random thickening of tone would spread through the tiles. Tiffany produced irregularities of surface to vary and enhance the qualities of light transmission. He was dissatisfied with the 'thin' colour being produced by most commercial glasshouses. He wanted the thick, dense colours of rubies and emeralds, or an indigo blue; he wanted mother-of-pearl, and cream and glimmering black.

Designs of dragons, rosettes and other plant forms, and abstract patterns were moulded on to some surfaces; and Tiffany, when fixing these tiles, would perhaps fit in a piece of ancient glass to evoke a movement of light in the opalescent surround. He longed to achieve the glittering faceted light of the Byzantines.

He had only his imagination as the ultimate guideline. He saw the colours, he felt the texture and variety of glass; he knew he could make it reality. But fantasies are hard to convey to others. He hints at the frustrations he experienced as he drove his glass workers to make what he saw in his mind. He told Charles de Kay that he was constantly trying to improve on his original ideas, and continued to learn, to his regret, that it was pointless making really beautiful windows unless he had total control of furnaces of his own. There is a hint here of the taskmaster. When he opened his own glasshouse in 1878, he employed a Venetian, Andrea Boldini, who, Tiffany facetiously remarked, 'represented himself as one of the workers in the Murano factory under Dr Salviati'. Boldini seems to have faded out of Louis' life after the glasshouse burnt down twice and Louis moved to the Heidt glasshouse. His debt to Boldini is never acknowledged, but Tiffany certainly learnt much from the Venetian and Louis' early vases show the influence of Murano designs. His work force expanded, as many designers and craftsmen were needed to produce the stained-glass window designs and the interior decorating. Louis himself played very little part in this latter aspect of his company. He was involved in the design and construction of all his glass work, but employed other designers to do interiors.

In 1888, he agreed to design the Ponce de Léon Hotel in St Augustine, Florida, and his decorations were greeted with high praise from the public and led to many more orders for the interior decorating department. Other artists murmured that Tiffany had betrayed his talent and opted for commercialism, as they watched his workshops flood the market with ever more fashionable windows, heavy in pictorial content and fruity in colour. John La Farge did not enjoy the same commercial success. He had been in demand, but his work, while popular in England, was no longer well received in the United States. Therefore, Louis Tiffany was not pleased when, on a trip to France in 1889, he found John La Farge exhibiting his stained-glass work to much critical acclaim. Tiffany went to talk to his friend, Samuel Bing.

The dealer in Oriental artefacts had become something of a guru to the young artists of France. His shop was a meeting place, and the Nabis often congregated there. He would be delighted to represent Tiffany in Europe. It was to be a lucrative relationship for both men.

In 1892, Tiffany dumfounded his critics when Bing exhibited a stained-glass window, *Four Seasons*. It was far removed from the popular designs Louis produced in such quantity in the United States and marked the arrival of Art Nouveau, years before the style reached its

Tiffany used tiles for some of his more daring experiments in glass, producing accidental effects that were lovely but often unrepeatable. Motifs – dragons, butterflies or abstract shapes – were stamped into the surface. Such tiles featured in many of his interior designs.

final maturity in Europe. Each of the four abstracted paintings symbolized a season and was decorated with brightly coloured borders. Tiffany relished the effect that *Four Seasons* had upon the critics and quickly became absorbed by another form of glass work. During his 1889 visit to Paris, when the La Farge exhibit had so irritated him, Louis saw the glass work of the remarkable furniture and glass designer, Emile Gallé of Nancy. The lovely engraved glass vases, with their free-flowing shapes, caught Tiffany's attention and his

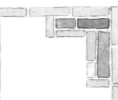

LEFT This 'Fish' mosaic, made in 1908, is a perfect example of Tiffany's artistic mastery. There is a modernity in his use of shapes and textures, an abstract quality far in advance of his time, yet perfectly suited to his material.

imagination. New visions of glass art were forming in his mind.

His creativity was yet to find its full expression. He was forty-two, and the father of six children – Louise had given birth to twin daughters and little Annie (who died as a small child). The Tiffany clan led a quiet life, divided between the city and the country. Charles Tiffany was now a venerable figure in New York and had been heaped with honours for his achievements by both royalty and his colleagues in the jewelry and silver

trades. In 1891, his family gathered together in Louis' studio to celebrate Charles and Harriet's golden wedding anniversary. The old man was justifiably proud of his wayward artistic son, even if he did not always understand him.

There was an eccentric mixture of shyness and showmanship in Louis. His daughters, in a published letter to Robert Koch, described the regularity of their father's domestic life. He was punctual, attentive and preferred to be at home with his plants, his children and

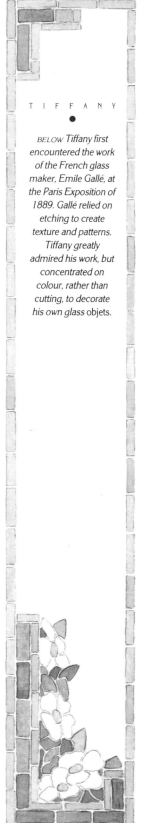

his beautiful objects. He adored music, but dreaded public concerts. He attended rehearsals of Gustav Mahler's work, but would hide from the orchestra. Alma Mahler told a story of how Louis even hid from guests in his own home.

Yet in his professional life, he was supremely confident and, as he aged, even arrogant. Tiffany, the imaginative, dedicated and productive artist, the reserved family man, was a superb salesman and promoter of himself and his products. He exhibited continually, and took to sending his work to take its rightful place in the great art museums of the world. He also took to giving public lectures, and dictated *The Artwork of Louis C Tiffany* to Charles de Kay. His lectures and his book are ardent and emotional but his words carry no analytical quality and fail to give us any further insight into his talent or the artistic era he inhabited. This is unfortunate, for Tiffany the glass maker proved to be a master of Art Nouveau.

LEFT *This stained-glass landscape, titled* Hudson River, *hints at the flat, decorative abstraction so typical of Art Nouveau. The plant forms assume an importance beyond their reality. But it was the rich, glorious colour that constantly identified the work of Tiffany.*

CHAPTER FIVE

PAINTINGS IN GLASS

*A brilliantly coloured mosaic section rescued from the
Philadelphia mint.*

Louis Comfort Tiffany may not have been a lucid writer, but this was not a weakness shared by other Art Nouveau artists. In fact, the movement is remarkable for the number of artist-poets it produced, and for its literary and scholarly fruit, which served to enlighten and engage disciples and the public alike.

This urge to put ideas into print was an inheritance from the leaders of the Arts and Crafts Movement: Owen Jones, William Morris and Walter Crane had been prolific writers, constantly putting pen to paper and hoping to educate public taste. A H Mackmurdo, the Scottish architect, was the first Art Nouveau designer to publish an art periodical, *The Century Guild Hobby Horse,* in 1884; *The Yellow Book* was instigated by Aubrey Beardsley. In Chicago *The Chap Book* appeared in 1894, and in Germany *Die Jugend,* in Barcelona *Jovendad,* and in Russia Diaghilev published *Mir Isskustua.* These periodicals talked of the aesthetics of art. The writers did not link their work to a social or religious philosophy and declared that artists were not meant to represent moral concepts. Art for art's sake was their cry.

James McNeill Whistler wrote poetry, and even literary figures like Oscar Wilde made their contribution. Wilde was also well paid for his lecture tour of the United States in 1882. He spoke on good interior design, and was influential in introducing new aesthetic ideas. Tiffany had met Wilde through his contact with MacKaye, and the Lyceum auditorium exemplified some of Wilde's notions on design. Candace Wheeler had entertained the famous writer in her studio.

However, the most prolific of writers and most effective teacher was the Belgian Art Nouveau designer, Henry Van de Velde. He was the principal of the design workshop at the Weimar Kunstgewerbeschule, under the patronage of the Grand Duke Wilhelm Ernst of Sachsen-Weimar from 1901 to 1914. Before he took up this appointment, he had worked in his native Belgium and in 1890 travelled to Paris, where he met Samuel Bing.

Van de Velde was concerned with the development of industrial design, and at the Weimar School he was to teach apprentices, not in the skill of creating one-off pieces but rather design for mass-production. Bing, despite his role as great entrepreneur of Art Nouveau ornament, *objets* and furniture, and his patronage of artists, was not averse to products made by machine. His main criterion was good and beautiful design, and he sold mass-produced items in his Maison de l'Art Nouveau shop only if they met his aesthetic standards.

The French Government sent Bing to the United States to undertake a survey of American art and

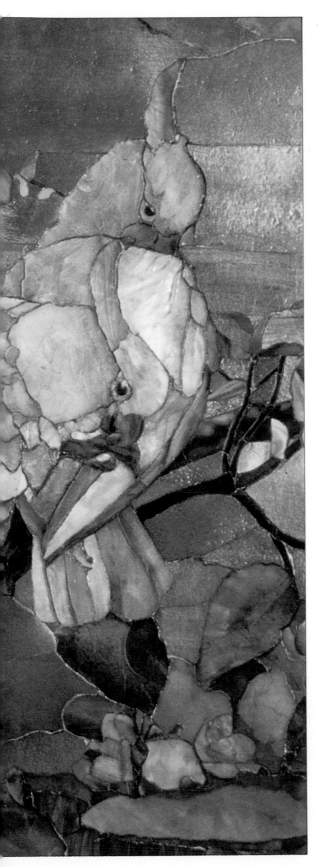

architecture. Bing was enormously excited by the industrial vigour he saw. Here, he felt, was fertile ground for radical growth in the world of industrial design. He wrote disparagingly of Old World attitudes to art and wondered at the non-commercial outlook of so many European artists. Things were different in the United States.

His host in New York was his friend Louis C Tiffany. Naturally, Bing was taken around the studios and workshops at 333 Fourth Avenue. Perhaps Louis guided him also through his father's establishment, where craftsmen were producing silverware and silverplate for Tiffany & Co. Bing was impressed by Louis' exploitation of the parallel skills of the artist and the artisan and his business organization, which supplied so many markets with such quantities of product. He reported that the Tiffany organization was a 'great art industry, a vast establishment combining under one roof, an army of artisans of all kinds united by a common current of ideas. It is perhaps by the audacity of such organizations that America will prepare a glorious future for its industrial arts'.[1]

His faith in Tiffany was not unfounded. Of course, Tiffany had a great belief in himself, too. He did not flounder in his many talents, but he did not give them a philosophical shape. An enterprise had grown by necessity, and almost unconsciously, around his creative energy. This had caused unfavourable comment from his fellow artists, and accusations of commercialism. Tiffany did not defend himself with theoretical argument. He simply created something so unusual, so original, that they were compelled to lower their critical voices. Bing articulated an ideal, a concept that gave the Tiffany enterprise a new shape and meaning and encouraged Louis to direct his talent into massproduction without loss of quality and status.

It is difficult to track the diverse activities and commercial success of Tiffany's life after 1890. There is Tiffany the stained-glass window designer, the maker of mosaics; Tiffany the industrial artist, with a studio of craftsmen and apprentices; Tiffany the creator of decorative glassware, and Tiffany the architect. An important commission in 1890 gave him the opportunity to demonstrate all his skills. His firm was asked to decorate the Havemeyer residence on Fifth Avenue. Louis Tiffany personally supervised the work, and the house was given his familiar theme of Islamic splendour with an eclectic mixture of ornaments, hanging lamps and carpets. But the extravagant mix was free of his youthful exuberance; a mature restraint prevented what might before have been passed off as confused self-indulgence. Contemporary accounts are breathless with admiration. Bing swooned. '*Nothing*

could achieve such a unified concept in an interior.'[2] Other reports noted that the sensational library ceiling was hung with a mosaic of multicoloured silks; Mrs Havemeyer was thrilled with the white mosaic hall and the pillars at the entrance to the gallery. Descriptions list Chinese embroideries, Viking designs and Celtic motifs in the woodwork, Japanese lacquers, carved gold mouldings and glittering mosaics.

It is impossible now, as we squint at black and white photographs, to grasp the splendour of these interiors. The famous 'hanging staircase' recalls a childhood memory of an 'Arabian Nights' illustration, although Mrs Havemeyer preferred to think it derived from the Doge's Palace in Venice. It is suspended between two levels and is constructed of metal, with spirals of metalwork encasing the basic struts; from these spirals, metal pendants hang in a filigree fringe. Numerous Oriental carpets lie across the floor, urns lurk in every corner, and filigree lamps, repeating the design of the fringed staircase, fill the air. Tiffany designed the interiors fully conscious of the Havemeyers' superb collection of paintings, including works by Rembrandt, El Greco and Manet.

The interior structural design may have been a model for British architects such as C F A Voysey and Charles Rennie Mackintosh; only Mackmurdo could have equalled it at the time. Certainly, contemporary artists who felt that Tiffany had tarnished his reputation with commercialism withdrew their charge after seeing the Havemeyer residence. Once again, he had surprised his critics with a fresh, unexpected creative approach.

Louis had persuaded Samuel Colman out of semi-retirement in Newport to help on this commission. He now left him to finish the details for the ecstatic Mrs Havemeyer, while he, Tiffany, hurried off to design a window at Yale University.

The university library had been donated a window by Samuel B Chittendon of Brooklyn, in memory of his daughter Mary Lusk. She had been the wife of William T Lusk, Tiffany's personal physician. The window size was intimidating – it measured 30 x 5 ft (9.14 x 1.52 m). Tiffany, with graceful ease, incorporated 20 figures into the design, linking them in a repetitive decorative motif. As was now the custom, the public lifted its voice in praise of the newest Tiffany window. 'It is truly a wonderful production from this man of thought' reported the Boston *Post*.

It was around this time that Bing visited the United States. He was to have a productive meeting with Tiffany, his host in New York. The two men enjoyed each other's company enormously. They shared a mutual admiration, even passion, for Japanese art.

CHAPTER FIVE
●

LEFT After his marriage to Louise Wakeford Knox, Tiffany won many ecclesiastical commissions. Churches across the United States were decorated with great stained-glass windows depicting Biblical scenes. This one is entitled Reading the Scrolls.

INSET The hanging staircase in the Havemeyer home was an ingenious design rendered in wrought iron. Although still richly decorated, this interior showed a new maturity in Tiffany's style.

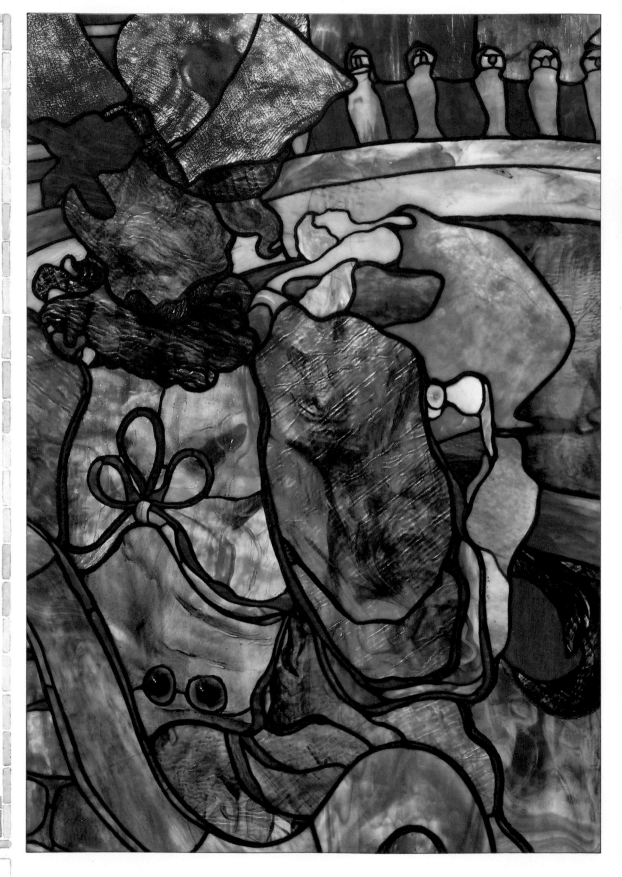

RIGHT *Tiffany
determined to create
stained glass that
reproduced the
tonalities of paint.
Samuel Bing
commissioned Henri
de Toulouse-Lautrec,
among other artists,
to paint a picture for
Tiffany. This is the
Lautrec painting
translated into stained
glass.*

FAR RIGHT *Mosaics were
used extensively in
this chapel designed
for the 1893 World
Fair in Chicago.
Tiffany created a
glittering Byzantine
interior within a
modern structure.
The building caused a
sensation.*

Bing appreciated that Tiffany did not need educating in the concepts of decoration and motif, as did so many others. During his visit, they planned an amazing project for Tiffany. Bing suggested that he commission some French artists to submit paintings that Tiffany would then execute in stained glass. The list of painters at Bing's disposal was impressive: Toulouse-Lautrec, Paul Ranson, Pierre Bonnard, Edouard Vuillard, Paul Sérusier, Henri Ibels, Ker-Xavier Roussel and Eugène Grasset were all involved. Tiffany treated this commission with due care, and great thoughtfulness. The painters presented a true test of his cherished ambition to make glass paintings without any tricks of marking or drawing on the medium. Sadly, most of these works – like so much of Tiffany's work – have been scattered, lost, hidden in private collections or even smashed up.

Tiffany felt no trepidation translating paintings onto glass. His early instinct for the abstract graphic in the mosaic system of stained glass was not relevant here. Some critics dismissed these glass works for this very deviation from the 'purist' approach to stained-glass work, and for the incongruity of mixing the media of paint and glass. They questioned, too, the relevance of opalescent glass. Tiffany was unconcerned by such arguments. Glass was a malleable, quixotic medium that did not have to justify its existence only by transmitting light. Other critics saw these works as a perfect statement of the Art Nouveau ethic – the ideal blending of fine art and applied art, and, in the glass maker's craft, they saw the ideal reduction of naturalism into decorative form. The windows were exhibited to much controversy at the Salon du Champs-de-Mars and then hung in Bing's new shop, La Maison de l'Art Nouveau, which opened in 1895.

The 1893 World Columbian Exposition in Chicago presented another showcase for Tiffany and many other Art Nouveau artists to display their wares. Louis originally planned to show six paintings as his contribution, but Bing persuaded him to present something grander. Tiffany designed a chapel.

The exhibition organizers had made no provision for stained-glass work, which needs special lighting and spatial resources, yet they were prepared to create the right environment for Tiffany. He did not finish it in time for the opening, and displayed it in New York before sending it to Chicago. Afterwards it was bought and donated to the Cathedral of St John the Divine in New York by a wealthy widow, Celia Whipple Wallace, and, finally, in 1916, returned to Tiffany. He then set it up in his house, Laurelton Hall, and declared it a chapel of art, not worship.

Tiffany's chapel extended into a 'light' room and a 'dark' room. Mosaics and marble were extensively used

and truly Byzantine light shimmered off the faceted, textured glass of these tessellated surfaces. As in the Havemeyer residence, the balance between the simplicity of structural line and luxurious detail showed a mature and sophisticated taste.

The 'light' room was hung with a chandelier of mother-of-pearl, whose light was reflected in silver and opal-coloured mosaic work. The 'dark' room was green and shifted in tone from a pale leaf-green to the navy-green of deep seawater. The chapel held a white marble altar, the façade of which was tiled in iridescent white mosaic. Blue and green mosaic peacocks, set in black marble, paraded the reredos. Romanesque arches contained the entire space, their column supports covered in mosaics of red, brown and green.

Again, contemporary critics praised the open pure lines of the chapel, saved from severity by the lavish surface ornament. Visitors loved its 'modernity' and were apparently unaware of any historical reference. Too little remains of the chapel for us to make a valid judgment, but verbal descriptions do *not* conjure up an image of 'modernity'.

Louis C Tiffany created these important works with his customary quick vitality and continued to look at other ways of working with glass. One report claims that he was simply looking for ways of using his spare glass; another that he was brooding on Emile Gallé's work in small *objets* made of glass. Whatever the motivation, Louis moved into a new dimension of glass work. In 1893, he acquired his own glasshouse, the

RIGHT *This advertisement for Samuel Bing's shop,* La Maison de l'Art Nouveau, *appeared in the German magazine* Dekorative Kunst *in 1898.*

FAR RIGHT *Tiffany's commercial success irritated his fellow artists and alienated some critics. This did not diminish his popularity. The public particularly admired his religious subjects.*

Corona furnaces on Long Island. More significant than this purchase, and the realization that he could experiment to please himself, was his meeting with Arthur J Nash. This Englishman had been trained in Stourbridge, Worcestershire where he had been a partner of the Whitehouse Glass Works before emigrating to the United States in 1892.

Arthur Nash was a technical expert and familiar with both modern English glass making techniques and traditional methods, and Tiffany employed him as chief designer and manager. Other employees were found quite easily as the Sandwich Glass Company in Massachusetts had just gone out of business, but Louis Tiffany relied upon the skill of his chief designer. It is doubtful that Louis could have extended his glass making techniques as dramatically as he did, without the technical knowledge of Arthur Nash.

Later, there were acrimonious reports over Tiffany's treatment of Arthur Nash, and of his deliberate denial of the contribution made by Nash to the glassworks. Douglas and Leslie Nash, Arthur's sons, accused Tiffany of trying to run the glassworks along philanthropic lines, thus bringing the company close to ruination; only their father's financial planning and commercial design skills had saved the Tiffany Glass and Decorating Co (the name of the business after 1894). It seems unlikely, for Arthur Nash stayed with Louis for more than 15 years and brought his sons into the business. The accusation that Tiffany wanted to run a philanthropic scheme at the glassworks is not supported by any other reference, save a report in A C Revi's *American Art Nouveau Glass.*

FAVRILE

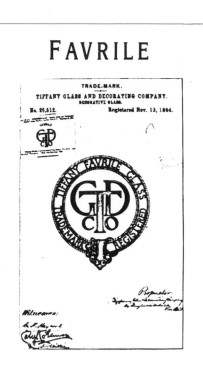

ABOVE Tiffany registered several trademarks. He designed two seals for his Favrile glass and in 1894 he registered a clearly marked logo for the Tiffany Glass and Decorating Company.

In 1894, Tiffany registered Favrile as a trademark, a name suggested, probably, by Arthur Nash. It is derived from the Old English 'fabrile', meaning belonging to the craft. Tiffany, the industrial artist, was launched; but so too was Tiffany the creator of Art Nouveau glass ornaments.

CHAPTER SIX
THE MESSAGE IN THE MEDIUM

This vase is a beautiful example of iridescent Millefiori glass.
Height 11 in (28 cm).

RIGHT A thick glass resembling marble was called Agate by Tiffany. This vase is blown and pattern moulded to achieve the desired effect. Height 11¼ in (28.5 cm).

Louis C Tiffany was at his most creative between 1893 and 1900, and made his own unique contribution to the Art Nouveau movement. He turned to 'small glass, and the production of a very popular, very varied and beautiful glass of novel quality'. The phrase is his own and while it is not modest, it understates his achievement.

In his glass ornaments, Tiffany expressed all the principles of Art Nouveau. As with his stained-glass windows, the medium carries within itself the material of the final image. Not a single line is drawn or painted onto the glass, because all tone and texture are contained within the material. In the glass ornaments, Tiffany extended even this frontier. He used the medium itself as the final image. The major characteristic of glass, its ductility, determined the shape and form of the image.

Tiffany's vases began life as balls of glass and were formed by the technique of glassblowing. A glowing ball of glass is withdrawn from the furnace and is slightly inflated with a tiny amount of air before being loaded by the glassblower at quite specific points with tiny amounts of glass of different colour and texture. The ball is effectively the vase in early embryonic form waiting for further inspirations of air to give it life. It is then returned to the furnace, withdrawn again and more glass is added. This process may be repeated as many as 20 times. All the different glasses so added, combined and variously manipulated, introduced originally as motifs, grow with the vase itself, and take

their place exactly as planned in advance in the mind of the artist. In this way, Tiffany infused the glass with decoration. He had his favourite motifs – the peacock feather, the iris, morning glories, gladioli, tendrils and trailing leaves. These were the motifs of Art Nouveau – essentially, organic forms abstracted into decorative surfaces and endowed with an asymmetrical linear quality.

In his *objets*, the seminal influence of Persian and antique Attic amphora can be discerned. When he was fully satisfied with the results of the experiments he carried out with Arthur Nash, Tiffany sent the results to Bing, who was astonished that 'after all the accomplishments of the Venetians, of Gallé and others, it was still possible to utilize glass in a new way that was often opaque and mat, with a surface like skin to the touch, silky and delicate'. (This tactile quality of slippery satin is characteristic of Favrile glass, and has not been exactly reproduced by any other glass maker.)

Tiffany contrived to have these glass ornaments shipped to France in time for the opening of La Maison de l'Art Nouveau and, of course, Bing displayed them. Art Nouveau had arrived.

Other exhibits included furniture from Van de Velde, paintings by Bonnard, Brangwyn, Pissarro and Toulouse-Lautrec, glass by Gallé, prints and drawings by Beardsley and Whistler, sculpture by Rodin. Louis Tiffany was represented by the 10 stained glass translations of paintings that Bing had commissioned, and some 20 pieces of ornamental glass. The opening proved Louis not only the foremost American exponent of Art Nouveau, but also a leader on the Continent. Afterwards, many glass workers were to imitate his creations.

Glass ornaments from the Tiffany furnaces were not presented for public sale until 1896. Only then did Louis feel that the design and quality had reached acceptable standards. He organized an exhibition of the work in his Fourth Avenue studios with invitations to the press to inspect his wares. The press were bewildered by the variety in design, colour and texture – and full of praise. Wherever the glass *objets* appeared, they were a success. In 1896, the Victoria and Albert Museum bought some pieces when they were put up for sale in the London branch of Tiffany & Co. Bing organized an exhibition, including the 10 stained glass windows, at the Grafton Galleries in London in 1899. The art periodical *The Studio* recorded its approval.

Louis also made pieces that he did not sell, as he considered them fine enough to be placed in museums. He made some extravagant claims that his ornamental glass had been delivered to museums all over the world – the Imperial Museum of Fine Art in

Tokyo, the Royal Museum in Berlin, as well as numerous American institutions. However, some of these museums deny that they received any collections from Tiffany, and say that the Favrile glass they have came from other benefactors.

The Favrile glass products are bewildering. Louis Tiffany was at his most creative on this small decorative level, and at his most prolific in his output. He not only fused decoration into the glass, he also allowed coloured abstracts to float through the material in a spontaneous gliding line. These latter pieces were known as 'accidentals', and attracted the attention of purists who saw them as the ultimate expression of the medium being the art form. On some vases he 'poured' a thick, meandering line over darkly opalescent glass, and called it Lava glass. Tiffany longed to capture the quality of antique glass, and in some of his attempts at its recreation, the texture, as if corroded by time, and the deep lustrous colour of great age, make his pieces almost indistinguishable from Roman glass. He called this Cypriote glass. There are thick marbled glasses, with colour streaming over and around the curved form.

As in his stained-glass work, Tiffany experimented with painterly, artistic effects. He achieved a curious realism in his nature designs. Flowers are pressed gently between layers of glass, or autumn leaves fall softly through opaque glass. Goldfish lurk in bowls of green glass, and peacock feathers weave a subtle pattern across the surface of a vase. He cut intaglio designs deep within the glass, leaving the surface

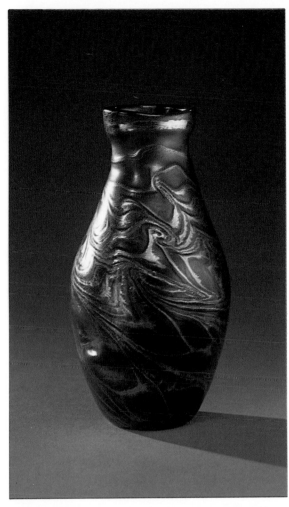

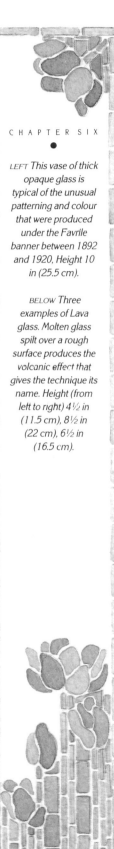

LEFT This vase of thick opaque glass is typical of the unusual patterning and colour that were produced under the Favrile banner between 1892 and 1920, Height 10 in (25.5 cm).

BELOW Three examples of Lava glass. Molten glass spilt over a rough surface produces the volcanic effect that gives the technique its name. Height (from left to right) 4½ in (11.5 cm), 8½ in (22 cm), 6½ in (16.5 cm).

unmarked. His most complicated technical achievement involved layers of glass combined with fused decoration. This glass is referred to as 'paperweight' or 'reactive' glass, and no other glass maker has sought to imitate it.

Favrile glass is divided into categories based on the various techniques employed to make it. A list of the categories, with a description of the technical methods, is presented at the end of this chapter.

There is also startling variety in the shapes Louis C Tiffany devised. Cecilia Waern, writing in *The Studio*, observed 'the shapes are often capricious but with all the sweet waywardness of this exquisite material; they are almost invariably simpler, less tortured and more classical, in the deepest sense, than the blown glass of Europe. They may recall shapes of Persia, Japan, Greece, because they have been *born* in the same way'. Nor must his colours be forgotten: the hard, brilliant, opalescent red; the shy, subtle greens carried against peacock-blue; navy-black with olive, overlaid with gold; clear Attic aquamarine; shimmering creams and oranges. Tiffany's response to colour was charged with emotion. He believed that colour is to the eye as music

is to the ear. He was not alone in the belief that there is a close correlation between colour and music. Musical forms were powerful leitmotifs in the works of other Art Nouveau artists. Whistler gave his paintings musical titles, *Nocturne in Blue & Green* and *Symphony in White*. Stravinsky wrote music to be seen through translation into ballet; Oscar Wilde said music was the ideal art, the only art that is essentially non-representational.

Tiffany also voiced his ideas on the relationship between colour and music, and, typically, the technician within him sought a scientific explanation. 'Today we are beginning to realize that ... light vibrations have a subjective power and affect the mind and soul, producing feelings and ideas of their own in the recipient brain. Light and sound are being studied in correlation .... Instruments are being invented to prove ... the subtle connection that exists between the two senses of colour and sound.'

Louis' ideas are better expressed in glass than in words. His emotions are articulated in the sinuous curve of a vase, the flowing line swirling in a waltz of red or gold or blue. His structures are full of movement, as sound is full of movement; the colours sing or murmur. In no better way could he express this synthesis of colour and sound; the great stained-glass windows are too complex, too full of other implications.

He produced his best material before 1900. Although he insisted, always, on his designs being carried through perfectly – he meticulously checked everything that left his glassworks – the popularity of the small glass objects was to force an ever-increasing supply to an eager public. Yet no identical pieces were made; each was individually designed and crafted, and several thousand Favrile glass objects were produced. By the time Arthur Nash left in 1919, with Tiffany's attention somewhat distracted by his last great project, Laurelton Hall, a certain stylish, indefinable element had gone.

FAR LEFT *A punch bowl of iridescent gold made from non-lead glass. Height 12½ in (31.5 cm)*

BELOW FAR LEFT *Favrile glass was most popular when Tiffany used an iridescent finish. This small glass bowl of amber carries an unusual indented design. Height 1 in (2.5 cm).*

LEFT *Organic forms were a constant motif in Art Nouveau. This glass representing an elegant flower form is made of blown lead glass. Height 16½ in (42 cm).*

RIGHT Peacock
feathers provide the
perfect pattern for an
iridescent Millefiori
vase with mass
appeal. Height 18 in
(45.5 cm).

There is much scholarly concern over the dating, numbering and signing of Favrile glass. Dating on a chronological basis is difficult, because there is no progressive change in style or method. Tiffany's markings followed an obscure reference system, which has not yet been unravelled. Sometimes, he signed a piece with his own initials, sometimes a company sign was used, and more often, an incomprehensible numbering system was applied.

It seems extraordinary that Tiffany permitted such an arbitrary approach. Accounts of his studios and glasshouse report a meticulous management of material, and a reference system that allowed a craftsman to find the exact colour and texture of a glass required in a mosaic or a window. In the basement in Corona, there were almost 300 tons of glass, classified into some 5,000 colours and varieties. His collection of domestic ware and artefacts was also carefully maintained. His *inro* were kept in specially designed chests for easy access. The studios were filled also with Chinese pots, Japanese boxes, Persian textiles and other artefacts, kept as reference material and as sources of inspiration for his designers and craftsmen.

There were many imitators of Favrile glassware. Louis Tiffany even sued a competitor, Frederick Carder. Carder first made his iridescent glass ornaments in 1904, copying many of Tiffany's shapes and even achieving a velvety texture by spraying them with stannous chloride. Carder established the Steuben Glass-

works in Corning, New York, and he registered his iridescent glass as Steuben glass. Tiffany started litigation in 1913, but as iridescent glass was a well-known process, Tiffany could lay no claim to its invention, and the matter was settled out of court.

There were glass makers who came very close to reproducing the Tiffany style. In Europe, there were numerous examples, but the most successful, in terms of close imitation, were made in Austria by Johannes Loetz Witwe of Klostermühle. These copies were being distributed around Europe as early as 1897 under the trademark 'Loetz Austria'. However, his range of colours was limited and he never achieved the silky tactile quality of Favrile glass. Tiffany spared no expense in his experiments, and could afford to be ahead of his competitors. If his range of colours and extensive experimenting gave Tiffany a lead in ornamental glassware, his distinctive designs, with their flair and sensual, organic movement, put him even further ahead.

There were other American houses working on glass ornaments, but, even if they did strive for the Tiffany effect, they marked their work and made no pretence of being Tiffany Favrile. These included the Quezal Art Glass and Decorating Company, and the Vineland Flint Glassworks. Much later, a pressed glass with a

LEFT Agate glass allowed for a sturdy, geometric use of the medium. Facets could be cut in a way not possible in other methods of production. These three objets demonstrate the qualities of this technique. Height (from left to right) 6 in (15 cm), 7½ in (19 cm), 4 in (10 cm).

RIGHT This blown vase, tall and shimmering, expresses the elegance of line that is a hallmark of Favrile glass. Here the Millefiori technique is used. Height 12 in (30.5 cm).

FAR RIGHT Such iridescent gold objets would later be copied in a vulgar form known as Carnival glass. The Jack-in-the-Pulpit vase FAR RIGHT was one of Tiffany's most successful designs and is a triumph of the glass maker's art. Height (from left to right) 10 in (25.5 cm), 19 in (48.5 cm).

sprayed-on iridescence of vulgar orange tones came onto the market. It was called Carnival glass and was the ultimate debasement of the extraordinary craft of glass work as developed by Louis Tiffany.

In 1900, Louis changed the name of his company to Tiffany Studios, as it was to remain until its closure in 1938. Tiffany Studios produced Favrile glass, stained-glass windows, mosaics, interior design, and numerous household goods.

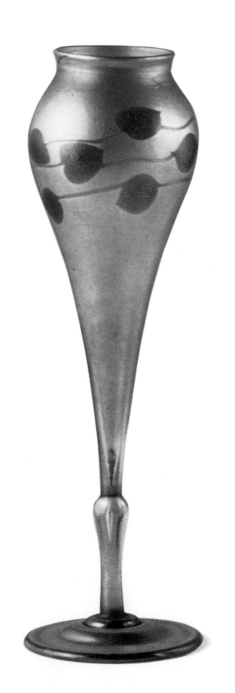

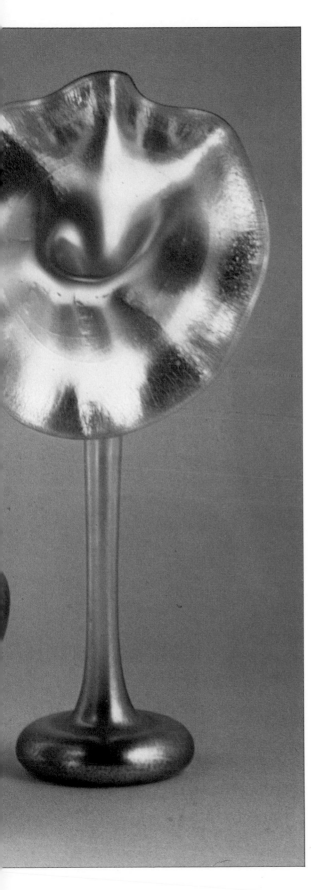

GLASS-MAKING TECHNIQUES AND TYPES OF FAVRILE GLASS

Although no two pieces of Tiffany glass are exactly similar, certain processes as described were in constant use. However simple these techniques may seem, their success depended on the consummate skills of the glassblower, who required a perfect knowledge of the materials with which he was working.

The glass used consisted of the traditional composition of sand (about 99% silica), soda-ash, potash, lead oxide and borax. The basic colours were achieved by adding various metallic oxides; blue glass from cobalt or cupric oxide, green from iron oxide, purple from manganese oxide, red from gold, copper or selenium, amber from carbonaceous oxides, iridescent yellow-green from uranium and black glass from a combination of manganese, cobalt and iron.

LUSTRE WARE

Lustre ware was first produced in Europe during the 1870s. Tiffany adopted the process and improved it so as to obtain a variety of subtle effects. In making these iridescent wares, salts of rare metals were dissolved into the molten glass and then kept in an oxidized state while the glass object was being made. It was then subjected to reducing flame, thus bringing the metallic coating to the surface. Finally, it was sprayed with another chloride. These salts reacted with the metallic surface, causing it to crackle into a mass of fine lines that reflect the light.

AGATE WARE

This was made by placing different-coloured opaque glass into one melting-pot and then mixing them until the mixture had the variegated appearance of agate or marble. Sometimes 'reactive glass' was also added to produce a laminated effect throughout. Agate ware objects had to be made quickly, and at a relatively low temperature, as excessive heat would turn the glass black.

CYPRIOTE GLASS

A 'gather' of yellow glass was rolled over a work surface covered with pulverized crumbs of the same glass; the encrusted surface of the object was then lustred.

LAVA GLASS

Basalt or talc was added to the molten glass, and the surface of the object was then gold-lustred.

RIGHT *The similarities of colour belie the varied production methods. The small lattice-work bowl is of Cameo glass, the decanter is marbleized, while the vase is Paperweight glass, a very difficult technique to master. All show seminal influences of ancient glassware in their design. Height (from left to right) 3 in (7.5 cm), 26 in (65.5 cm), 13 in (33 cm).*

●

LEFT With these aquamarine objets, Tiffany acknowledged his debt to antique glass. Naming them the 'Tel el Amarna' vases, after the excavation of Pharaoh Amenhotep IV's capital, he retained the simple shape of the Egyptian original while producing a more brilliant colour tone. Height (from left to right) 7 in (18 cm), 15 in (38 cm), 6 in (15 cm).

RIGHT Cutting the intaglio patterns on these vases was a slow and laborious craft. Such work, though skilled, does not convey the flowing, subtle movements of other Favrile techniques. Height (from left to right) 12 in (30.5 cm), 20 in (56 cm), 11¾ in (30 cm).

FAR RIGHT ABOVE The lustre, which Tiffany constantly sought to achieve in his work, attains a metallic quality in this small iridescent bowl.

FAR RIGHT BELOW Tiffany did not perceive glass as a smooth, translucent material. Here the material is blown into whorls and eddies that set up new tones of colour through the varying depth of glass. Height 4 in (10 cm).

PAPERWEIGHT OR REACTIVE GLASS

This term is applied to all translucent Tiffany glass that has changed colour and become iridescent when reheated in the furnace. Internal decoration, in the form of flowers and abstract organic shapes, was often created in this medium.

CAMEO GLASS

This was the only type of Tiffany glass decoration not to be produced while the glass was semi-molten. The engraving of glass with fine scraping tools and grinding-wheels had been practised since ancient times. The skill enjoyed a considerable revival in England and France during the late 19th century, and the technique was quickly adopted by Tiffany. Working the glass is a slow and laborious task requiring great ability and patience on the part of the craftsman.

MILLEFIORI GLASS

This had been produced as early as the 2nd century BC although the process was not revived until the mid-19th century. The decoration is composed of sections of glass rods containing the form of the desired motif, usually a flower. The pattern passes through the whole length of the rod, rather like the lettering in a modern stick of 'rock' (rock candy). Wherever the desired decoration was to appear on the finished article, a small round patch of opalescent glass was applied to the object and then touched with the end of the glass rod. When the rod was detached a narrow cross-section would remain fused to the opalescent glass patch. The whole object was then reheated and the applied flowers were moulded into the body of the vase, where they struck various shades of purple, red, blue and white.

©Haworth Art Gallery, North Western Museum and Art Gallery Services, England.

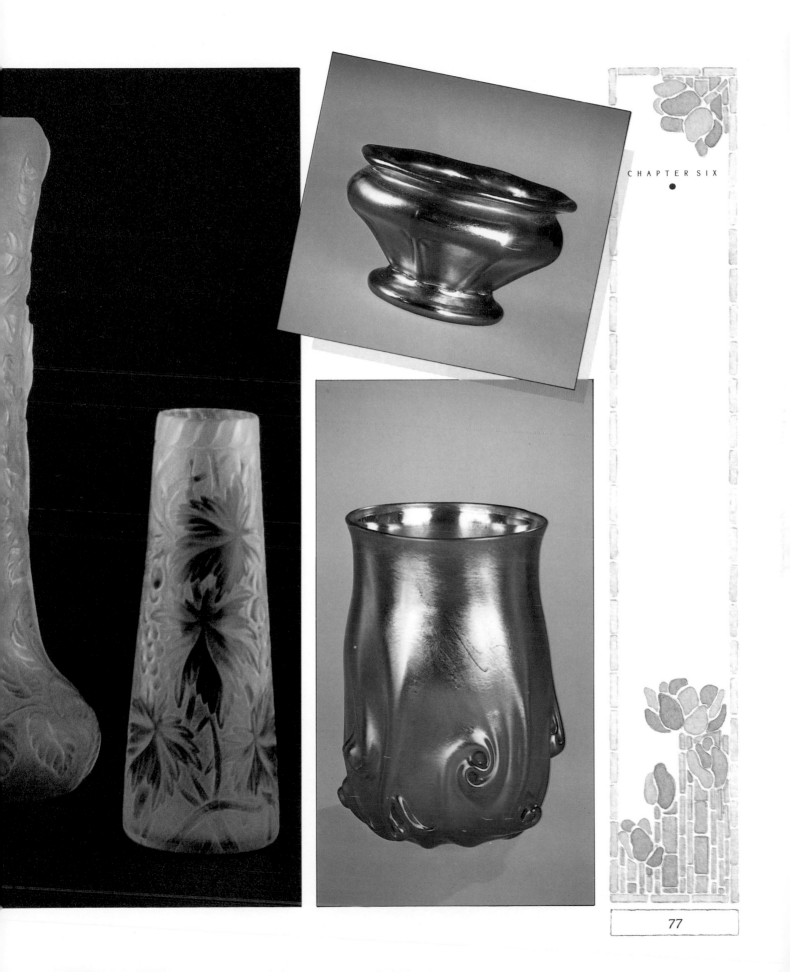

ABOVE RIGHT Three iridescent vases with free-flowing organic designs in the rich indigo blues and golds that Tiffany Studios made so popular. Height (from left to right) 8 in (25 cm), 6 in (15 cm).

BELOW RIGHT This punch bowl of iridescent glass and gilded silver was made for the Paris Exposition of 1900. Height 14½ in (37 cm), circumference 24 in (61 cm).

*LEFT Four objets
made using the
Paperweight
technique. The
central pair carry the
Autumn Leaf pattern.
Height (from left to
right) 8 in (20.5 cm),
17 in (43.5 cm), 4 in
(10 cm), 8 in
(20.5 cm).*

RIGHT *Transparent iridescent gold and blue glass; blown. Height 14 in (35.5 cm).*

MIDDLE *This representational goldfish bowl is one of Tiffany's more curious designs. Extremely difficult to execute, it was not often repeated. Height 15 in (37.5 cm).*

FAR RIGHT *Another in the popular Jack-in-the-Pulpit series. Tiffany made numerous versions using various colour effects. Height 19 in (48.5 cm).*

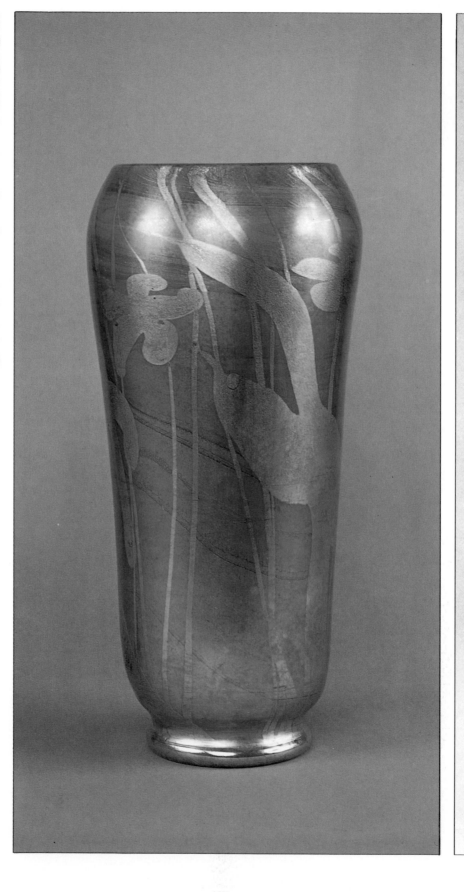

ABOVE RIGHT AND MIDDLE Art Nouveau's swirling lines transformed reality into a decorative symbol. In his glass ornaments, Tiffany's plant forms flow through the medium and become rhythmical designs of subtle colour. Height (from left to right) 5 in (13 cm), 5 in (13 cm).

BELOW RIGHT These three small iridescent vases reproduce the typical shapes of Roman glassware. Height (from left to right) 3 in (8 cm), 4½ in (11 cm), 6 in (15 cm).

●

LEFT AND BELOW LEFT
Having perfected the production of stained glass to achieve texture and tonality without the use of paint, Tiffany employed a number of techniques to create a bewildering variety of small glass ornaments. Height (from top to bottom) 7 in (18 cm), 9 in (23 cm), 4¾ in (12 cm).

CHAPTER SEVEN

THE ART INDUSTRY

This lamp illustrates Tiffany's skills as both a glass maker and a metal worker. The curved shape of the shade is repeated in ornate metal worked over the glass base.

Louis C Tiffany's Favrile glass ornaments, particularly those produced before 1900, have been the subject of considerable research. These *objets* alone have ensured Tiffany's place in the history of art.

Tiffany the industrial artist has aroused less interest. He was not an elitist in his artistic outlook and was glad to observe that 'industrial art comes nearer to the people'. He regarded the industrial wealth of his country and its evidence in lavish public and private expenditure with satisfaction. 'Already' he said, 'are legislative halls, railway stations and opera houses liable to be . . . more beautiful than the palaces of the rich.'

Tiffany Studios contributed an enormous range of household goods to service the demand for beauty in the home. The most famous of these are the lamps, a natural outlet for Tiffany's interest in glass and the effect of light on colour. He had designed a fantasy of lighting, matching his gas-lit sconces against a background of mosaic in the White House in 1882. The Lyceum Theater had brought him to the harshness of electricity. These designs, and the lighting fixtures for the Havemeyer house, had been worked in bronze. And the 'hanging staircase' was also metal work. This was the material he applied to ornamentation in the Seventh Regiment Armoury, one of his first interior decorating commissions.

Louis Tiffany held a comprehensive knowledge of the effects of light, transmitted and reflected. He considered the harsh brightness of electricity, and softened the glare with lovely colour. He also gave technical consideration to his design. The electric lamps were given armatures to alter the focus of light. Shades could be interchangeable. Tiffany combined function with aesthetic appeal in these lamps.

Tiffany started to sell his lamps in 1895, although they had been exhibited earlier in the Women's Building at the World's Fair in 1893. His former colleague, Candace Wheeler, was President of the Women's Building. Perhaps Louis' early professional relationship with Mrs Wheeler and the Society of Decorative Art in New York had taught him that craftsmanship knows no gender limitations. A number of major women designers emerged from his studios, and he was fair and generous in training and paying these employees. His two major designers in the department of lamps were Mrs Curtis Freschel and Clara Driscoll.

Mrs Freschel designed the famous Wisteria Lamp, and Clara Driscoll developed patterns for the Ivy, Rose, Geranium and Butterfly lamps, among numerous others. The leaded glass shades were not an innovation from the Tiffany Studios, but his designs were far superior to any other similar product. It is forgivable to

RIGHT Tiffany seized the opportunity to create ornamental bases for his lamps. The restrained simplicity of the bulbs in this Pond Lily lamp contrasts with the intricacy of the base. This design won a Gold Medal at the 1902 Turin Exposizione.

●

LEFT The beautiful
simplicity of the
slender base provides
the perfect foil for the
gorgeous colours of
the dragonfly shade in
this standing lamp.

think of Tiffany lamps primarily in terms of the coloured patterns of stained glass, but the stands and the bases are also significant. Under Tiffany's transforming hand, the bronze bases became works of art.

Byzantine designs were sometimes used, and an antique appearance given by the use of mossy green colours. The organic shapes of nature – leaves, tendrils, cobwebs, roots of trees – became models for curving, sculptural forms. Tiffany moulded abstract patterns, with bronze lines curling around space. He set glass balls into the spaces, delighting in the colour alteration when the lamps were lit. The leaded glass shades assumed the natural forms of branches and fruit and flowers; or the circular spread of wings and spider's webs. Their titles confirmed their origin and form – Pansy, Orange Petal, Snail, Queen Anne's Lace. All were realized in the jewel-like colours of Tiffany's stained glass. At the Turin Exposizione in 1902 the Wisteria Lamp won an award.

His standing lamps are remarkably functional and modern in design. One example is a tall bronze column, set upon angled legs, which has a globe constructed of metal strips between which black glass is set. The light is transmitted in a greenish shimmer. It was purely functional in its shape, and gains its decorative status from the unusual lighting.

Before 1900, the lamps were marked with the logo 'The Tiffany Glass and Decorating Co', and thereafter, 'Tiffany Studios New York'.

Pattern moulds were made so that the same lamps could be reproduced again and again, and made in various sizes. So widely popular did this style become in the United States that a 'Tiffany lamp' is now a generic term for lamps with stained-glass shades.

*LEFT An extravagant
arrangement of leaves
and fruit tumbles over
the shade of this
Grapevine lamp,
supported by a plain
stem simulating the
texture of wood.*

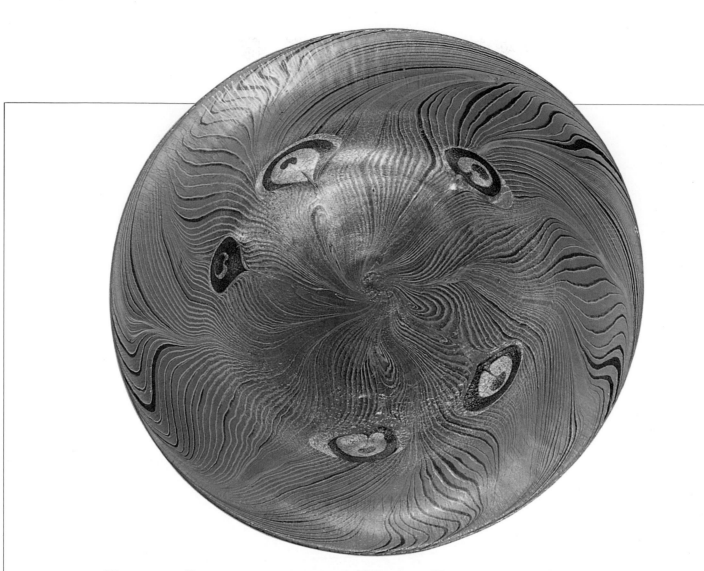

MASS-PRODUCTION FROM TIFFANY STUDIOS

Furniture and 'quality reproductions' were supplied by Tiffany Studios. Drapes, textiles, carpets and rugs were also on offer. Tiffany described these aspects of his business in *The Artwork of Louis C Tiffany*. '[He] has been tempted to make excursions into the field of the loom through the charm of textile work, in order to obtain rugs, carpets and hangings which will express his particular colour sense and harmonize with certain given interiors. While he has never set up looms of his own, he has devoted a good deal of time to the dyeing and finishing of textiles woven elsewhere, taking looms of

neutral shade and giving them art value .... In this way he has made them vie with paintings for their color charm ... and surpass paintings in ... decorative effect.'

Tiffany Studios also manufactured a remarkable range of decorative and purely functional items for the home. Simple objects used in daily domestic life were another successful side of Louis Tiffany's business. Bonbon dishes, marmalade jars, cologne bottles, cups, plates, tobacco jars, cigar lighters, cigarette cases, pin cushions, finger bowls, decanters and salt cellars were but a few of the utensils available from the Studios. Desk

sets of glass, bronze and mother-of-pearl were created; jewellery boxes; dinner services – the list goes on. Some were extremely costly, worked as they were with precious metals and gems; other items were quite inexpensive. All Tiffany goods nonetheless enjoyed a certain chic and their range was always increasing. '[I have] for some time been carrying on elaborate experiments in enamels and pastes, applied to ... lamp bodies, boxes, vases and the like', he said. Tiffany eventually opened an enamel department under the supervision of Julia Munson. She, and other designers, have described Tiffany's

working methods. He would sketch his idea for a designer, but only the basic structural shape. The designer would have the responsibility of choosing materials and colours. At their disposal was, of course, the varied and exotic collection of treasures. Tiffany was also in the habit of taking selected craftsmen on trips abroad to broaden their artistic horizons. There is an apocryphal story that one worker was sent to the Caribbean and instructed to stay there for a year to study the colour of the sea and capture the exact tones in glass. Tiffany claimed that he checked every item of Favrile glass.

ABOVE LEFT *The essence of Art Nouveau is perfectly expressed in this Favrile plate. Its lines radiate in a swirling rhythm.*

ABOVE *Tiffany practised pottery, in which he again sought unusual colour effects. This ceramic flask has a thick, creamy texture of typical subtlety.*

ABOVE RIGHT *Tiffany Studios' interior design service extended to the provision of all fixtures and fittings for the home. This ashwood chair with marquetry inlay was manufactured in the Tiffany workshops.*

BELOW RIGHT *Such household items as this enamelled box were so popular as gift purchases that they became known as 'wedding-gift Tiffany'.*

RIGHT *The Gould Peacock lamp is one of Tiffany's more bizarre designs. It is made of Favrile glass, with enamel work over a copper base. Height 40½ in (103 cm).*

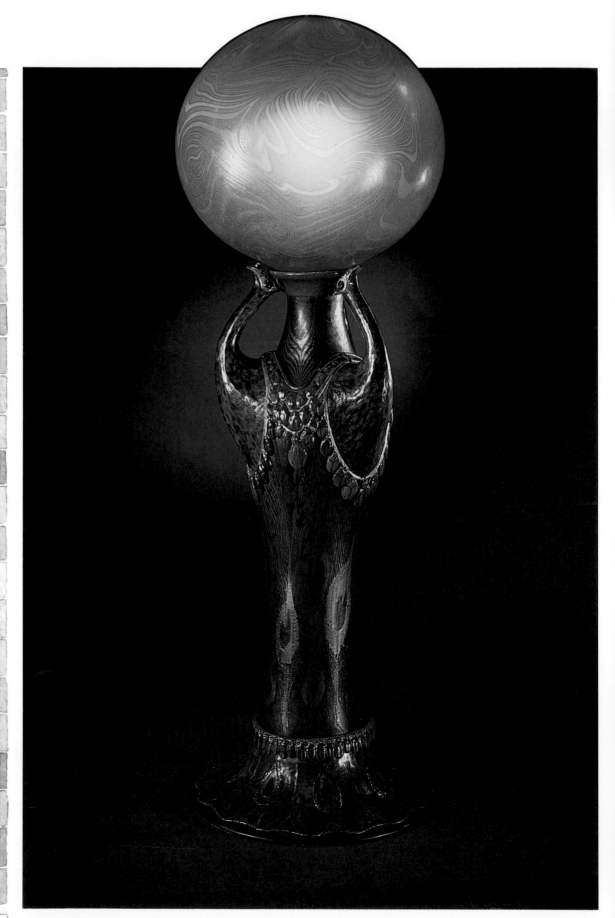

LEFT The sculptured metal base provides a sturdy, yet stylish, accompaniment for the Rose Bower glass shade of this lamp made in 1900. Height 24 in (61 cm).

RIGHT *The famous Wisteria lamp, designed by Mrs Curtis Freshel, was an enduring favourite from the Tiffany workshops.*

Louis, having exhausted bronze as a medium, turned to ceramics as another material from which to construct his lamp bases. The tactile quality of clay, the different colours produced by firing, excited him. Some of his ceramic work was extremely beautiful, and although it is not as widely known as his glass work, there are some remaining pieces, much-prized rarities in private collections and a few museums.

Louis Tiffany took design into ordinary homes and, in his way, shaped the taste of the United States. His organization of the assembly line and skilled craftsmen brought 'art to the people'. In this achievement he is closer to Arthur Lasenby Liberty than to William Morris.

Liberty infuriated the Arts and Crafts Movement by manufacturing moulds for mass-production that gave his metal ware a 'hand-beaten' look. Poor Morris, whose achievements were universally influential, confronted by the high cost of his beautiful handcrafted products and the limited market they therefore reached, was exasperated by having to 'minister to the swinish luxury of the rich.' Tiffany had no such qualms.

In the 1890s, Tiffany bought another home, a country estate on Long Island, where the family spent their summers. Tiffany designed and decorated the interior. The furniture was made to his specifications by the Millbank House in Connecticut. 'The Briars' was

FAR LEFT This table lamp is unusual in that the geometric lead strips, not the colour, dominate the design.

LEFT The date of manufacture of this rare ceramic table lamp, like many Tiffany products, is uncertain. Made between 1895 and 1910, its mix of colour and brass detail is a delight.

a surprising departure from the opulent Oriental style. The furniture has a severe functional appearance and shows the influence of the simple, heavy furniture made by the Shaker Community. This religious sect rejected modern production techniques and retained an austere design in their furniture. The interiors in The Briars have a bare, spacious appearance, and the surface details are delicate and unobtrusive. Ornaments and furniture were placed with a sense of unity and proportion. The lamps were the most decorative element. Tiffany also laid out a flower garden, which gave him much pleasure, and which he guarded fiercely from marauding children and guests.

TIFFANY JEWELRY

Jewelry designed by Tiffany was produced under the auspices of Tiffany & Co. However, the art jewelry department, opened in the store, was not financially viable and had to be closed.

ABOVE Tiffany mixed opals with translucent glass in this necklace, but unlike his contemporaries he did not submerge the gems in their setting.

LEFT Tiffany liked the hard, clear design of Romanesque jewelry. The necklace depends upon the strong colour of aquamarine stones and its silver setting is unobtrusive. The enamel brooch's organic design places it closer to the Art Nouveau ethic.

In 1902 Charles Tiffany died aged 90. Charles T Cook became President of Tiffany & Co for a few years. In 1907, John C Moore, son of Edward, assumed his position. Louis was Vice-president, and art director to the company. Tiffany & Co were by now world famous for their jewelry. Charles Tiffany had collected an enormous store of precious stones over the years. His craftsmen used these gems in designs for sword scabbards, tiaras and coronets. Louis opened an 'art jewelry' department in the store,

and Julia Munson was appointed as supervisor. The pieces created by Louis himself were marked 'Tiffany & Co' like all the others, making verification of his designs difficult. He was able to use the most precious stones – diamonds, emeralds, rubies, amethysts and opals – and, of course, he did. The pieces were perhaps too expensive, though, and the art jewelry department was not entirely successful. It was closed in 1916.

Many Art Nouveau designers created jewelry, Henri Van de

Velde, René Lalique and A H Mackmurdo among them. Their pieces strove to achieve an organic–symbolic arrangement, the metal and the stone confused in contorted lines. Robert Melville in *The Anti-Rationalists* describes Art Nouveau jewelry as soft jewelry, because both jewel and metal are made to look malleable, even limp. Tiffany's jewelry did not always have this soft effect. Quite often the stones retained their hard, gemstone quality, while the metal supported them firmly within a decorative line.

LEFT The Briars was Tiffany's first country home and its interiors were more functional than those of his city apartments. Embellishments to the Colonial-style parlour were limited to intricate ceiling lamps and an Oriental carpet.

Tiffany was to involve himself closely with three more commissions for Tiffany Studios, but over the next few years, he concentrated on his family and his own projects. He employed Joseph Briggs to manage the business for him. Briggs, an Englishman from Accrington in Lancashire, had worked for Tiffany since 1890. He was to run the furnaces until they closed in 1928 and Tiffany Studios until his death. He never lived in England again, but sent his family a quantity of Tiffany glass. This collection, the finest single collection in Europe, was later donated by the Briggs family to the Haworth Art Gallery in Accrington.

After his father's death, Louis C Tiffany went into a flurry of house-buying. He purchased the apartment-mansion on 72nd Street from his father's estate. Tiffany moved his studios from Fourth Avenue into a building on 45th Street at Madison Avenue and he bought a resort hotel on 580 acres of land at Oyster Bay, Long Island. This property, Laurelton Hall, was to be an extraordinary testament to his creativity – displaying his virtuosity in architecture, interior design, glass work and painting.

LAST CAUSES

A fantasy of medieval warfare was created in stained glass for the
American Red Cross headquarters in Washington DC.

 The old hotel on Oyster Bay was demolished, and builders started work on the house designed by Tiffany. It was to be years before it was completed, partly because of litigation by the previous owner, and partly because Louis kept adding to the place. In 1905, however, it was ready for habitation.

Louise Tiffany died in 1904. Once again, Louis found himself with motherless children. Four of his daughters were at home – Hilda, from his first marriage, the twins Julia and Comfort who were 17 years old, and Dorothy who was 13. His eldest daughter was married to Graham T Lusk, and Louis gave them The Briars as a home. His son Charles was at Yale University, being groomed for a position in Tiffany & Co.

Memories of his first widowhood, when Tiffany had indulged in a brief whirl with some chorus girls, were unpleasantly revived by a shocking event in 1906. His friend Stanford White had never quite outgrown his penchant for young chorus girls and fell in love with a teenage actress, Evelyn Nesbitt. Evelyn married, and her husband, out of jealousy, shot Stanford White dead during a performance in the Madison Square Theater. Tiffany reacted by being very strict with his daughters, and unkind to their suitors. He distracted the girls with long trips abroad and tennis parties at home. But all his daughters were soon to leave him. Julia married Gurdon Parker, an architect, in 1910; Comfort became Mrs Robert de Kay Gilder in 1911, and Dorothy married in 1914 Dr Robert Burlingham. Sadly Hilda died of tuberculosis in 1909.

Louis' move to Oyster Bay was not smooth. He squabbled with his neighbours over electricity and beach rights, and they suspected him of affairs with other men's wives. Theodore Roosevelt was a neighbour, and perhaps he expressed his feelings when he smashed the White House screen.

Laurelton Hall absorbed much of his energy. It was a project to last him the rest of his days. The architecture was quite extraordinary, a great fantastic dream of the Tiffany imagination brought to life. The familiar influences were there – Byzantine, Islamic, Romanesque – but there were departures from these sources, innovations made by nobody else before. Tiffany was not formally trained as an architect, and he built a clay model to illustrate his plan. The house was designed on various elevations, and the lay-out was asymmetrical, as befitted a great Art Nouveau artist. It has been described as the largest and most important achievement of Art Nouveau in America. The building was centred on a courtyard through which a stream meandered. There was a fountain that was a tall, glass vase in the shape of a Green amphora. This fountain was only one of seven. Another was a life-size model of Venus. Tiffany engineered a system of water reticulation, so that the water flowed constantly, splashing through the fountains and into several ponds, before running into an underground pipe that fed it back to the stream and fountains. The pools and fountains were decorated with exotic plants.

Tiffany designed rooms to express the different moods of light. Leading off the courtyard, was a 'dark' room, the living room – shadowed, dim and sheltered. The cornices were curved into the ceiling, and the fireplace, deep and wide, was dropped below the floor level. Stained-glass windows filtered the light, and mosaics glimmered on the walls.

Also leading off the central court was a 'light' room, the dining room – bright, airy and open. Tiffany placed huge plate glass windows from floor to ceiling, opening the room at one end to the sea, and at the other, to the garden. He created an illusion of living in nature. Clear glass had never been used in such a way before, and it presaged other technical advances in modern American architecture. At the far end of the courtyard, the stream formed a pool in which sat a giant rock-crystal. Tiffany built an elevated terrace from which the view of Cold Harbor Bay could be fully enjoyed.

He created rooms to suit his *objets d'art* – a Chinese room, an American Indian room, and so on. There were 84 rooms and 25 bathrooms in Laurelton Hall.

It is impossible to imagine this mansion. Yet again, we have to rely on photographs, because Laurelton Hall was burnt to the ground in 1957. This last house by

FAR LEFT The uncluttered lines of the octagonal table and wide lamp harmonize with the spatial qualities of the 'light' dining room in Laurelton hall.

LEFT Laurelton Hall, showing the great rock crystal in the pool and the stepped garden of exotic trees leading up to the house.

BELOW LEFT The central court surrounded a fountain in the shape of a Greek amphora. A portrait of Tiffany painting in his beloved garden was displayed in this room.

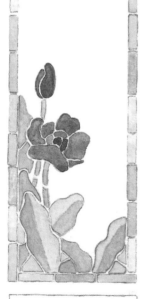

RIGHT *Though
Laurelton Hall has
been described as a
supreme example of
Art Nouveau
architecture, its
angular lines strike a
modern note. It is a far
cry from the sinuous
glories of Gaudi,
maestro of the mode,
whose Casa Mila in
Barcelona is shown
here.*

FAR RIGHT *Exterior and
interior of Laurelton
Hall. The living room
below was conceived
as a 'dark' room. Light
filtered through
stained-glass
windows and the
decor was ornate. The
Bathers, one of
Tiffany's last works in
glass, can be seen in
the rear.*

Tiffany took five years to build at a cost, in 1908, of half a million dollars.

In 1909, he designed a stained-glass drop curtain for the National Theatre in Mexico City. This was a mammoth project. A team of 20 workmen took more than 15 months to complete it and when finished it comprised nearly a million pieces of glass weighing 27 tons. Louis sent the painter Harry Stoner to Mexico, to make sketches of the local landscape, flora and fauna. Stoner produced a vista of the Valley of Mexico as seen from the President's Palace. Snow-capped mountains, a lake, trees and a cactus were translated into glass.

Tiffany Studios continued to service orders for major stained-glass windows, mainly in churches. Louis had sketched the ideas for wonderfully rich coloured, faceted glass constructed in circles, like great medallions. These were installed in the Old Blandford Church in Petersburg, Virginia and the Christ Congregational Church in Fairfield, Connecticut. The Red Cross asked for three memorial windows in their Washington headquarters. Louis' last personal venture into ecclesiastical windows was in a Brooklyn church in 1916, but it too was destroyed in a fire.

LEFT Water was an important element in the design of Laurelton Hall. Pools and fountains were scattered throughout the interior and exterior. A life-size Venus served as a fountain.

RIGHT *Further scenes from the Red Cross commission. The women and their burdens were intended to symbolize the aims of the organization.*

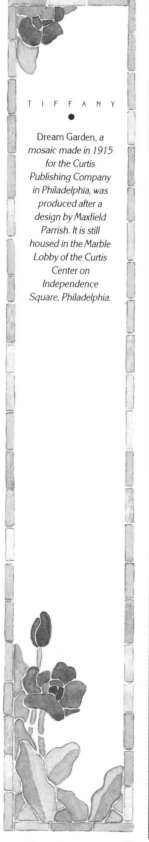

Dream Garden, *a mosaic made in 1915 for the Curtis Publishing Company in Philadelphia, was produced after a design by Maxfield Parrish. It is still housed in the Marble Lobby of the Curtis Center on Independence Square, Philadelphia.*

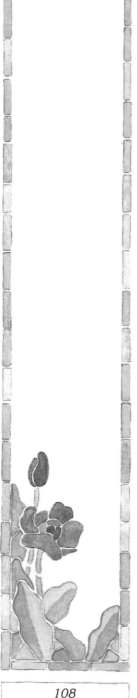

In 1911, the Curtis Publishing Company requested a glass vista for their new building in Philadelphia. Three designers had been asked to submit sketches, but, oddly, all died before they could do the work. Tiffany was delighted to have the commission, but could not provide a suitable sketch. Maxfield Parrish was eventually approached and after six months of discussion agreed on a design with Tiffany, with the nervous patron hoping meanwhile that they, too, would not die prematurely. A year later the mosaic was finished, the artists were still alive, and the public loved it.

Dream Garden is 15 ft/1.5 m high and 49 ft/14.7 m long and nowhere better described than by Tiffany himself, writing in a brochure produced by the Curtis Publishing Company. 'In translating this painting so that its poetical and luminous idealism should find its way even to the comparatively uneducated eye, the medium used is of supreme importance . . . . Selecting the lustrous, the transparent, the opaque and the opalescent, each with its own texture, a result is secured [in glass] which does illustrate the mystery, and it tells the story, giving play to the imagination, which is the message it seeks to convey . . . . I trust it may stand in the years to come for a development in glass-making and its application to art which will give to students a feeling that in this year of nineteen hundred and fifteen something worthy has been produced for the benefit of mankind.'

Dream Garden did stand in the years to come. It was neither burnt, nor smashed up, but is still part of the Curtis Publishing House building in Philadelphia, although its proprietors have changed.

Tiffany, however, was under siege. Perhaps he was driven to defend this last great mosaic in these extravagant terms, for the artistic world was changing and Tiffany was no longer in the avant-garde. His

glorious chapel, designed and built for the World's Fair in 1893, and installed for posterity in the Cathedral of St John the Divine, was sealed off in darkness. This desecration happened in 1911 under instruction from the architect, Ralph Adam Cram. Cram was a member of a new school that loathed the rich, vibrant stained glass of the previous generation. He had designed the Russell Sage Memorial Chapel in Far Rockaway, Long Island, and planned to insert simple clear stained glass in the neo-Gothic windows but instead a Tiffany design had been accepted. Cram was furious, and when he was architect on the building and refurbishment of St John the Divine, took his revenge. Tiffany removed the chapel for display at Laurelton Hall.

Louis C Tiffany was not easily discouraged. The Parrish painting for *Dream Garden* had inspired him. He painted his own picture and transformed it into glass and *The Bathers* was hung in the living room of

Laurelton Hall. This exercise took Louis Tiffany back to the art of painting. All his life, he had made watercolour sketches of buildings and flowers, and for his interior designs. Now, he took up oils again. He also revived his abiding theatrical interest, and determined to stage his own dramatic event.

Tiffany issued invitations to several hundred people to attend an Egyptian Fête on 4 February 1913 at his 72nd Street studio. He hired an Egyptologist, John Lindon Smith, who had painted excavations, to design the party. The invitations were issued on simulated papyrus rolls, and told the guests to appear in costumes of Cleopatra's era. Catering was by Delmonico's. The performers of an Egyptian masque were 'socialite amateurs' and family. The studio was set to look like the banks of the Nile, and the Philharmonic Orchestra lurked in a recess. Two professionals, Ruth St Denis and Paul Swann, popular dancers in New York, performed to music composed for the occasion by Theodore Steinway. (Years before Louis had decorated Steinway pianos.) Tiffany's official excuse for this extravaganza was to present a scenario that would bring his guests to an understanding of 'art'. The party was a riot, a revelry of champagne and music, and the social columns of the newspapers raved at the success of this lavish event.

On the next day, a less glamorous event opened in the 69th Regiment Armory. It probably passed unnoticed by the socialites, but the Armory Show was a deeply significant art exhibition, and it marked the passing of the Art Nouveau era. Tiffany noticed it and was confused: the paintings and sculpture did not represent beauty as he understood it. It introduced the Post-Impressionists to America and was sponsored by a new group, the Association of American Painters and Sculptors. The new French schools were represented by Fauvism, Cubism and Orphism. There was fierce debate on Duchamp's *Nude Descending a Staircase,* in which the figure is reduced to geometric cubes, with angular lines to express movement.

In 1912, Louis had dictated his life work and achievements to Charles De Kay. In 1914, he had the text published privately in a limited edition. *The Artwork of Louis C Tiffany* had chapters headed 'Tiffany the Painter', 'Tiffany the Maker of Stained Glass', 'As Landscape Painter' and so on. Tiffany was unaware of the florid tone of his words, but even his powerful ego understood how remote contemporary art was from his own work.

The Armory Show exhibits were, for him, an attack on his aesthetic world. He hated them, he thought they were ugly and he could and would not admit that they were new, fresh or progressive.

RIGHT Tiffany Studios lost their design leadership after the Armory Show and were destined to gradually wither under the onslaught of Modernism. Yet Louis C Tiffany retained the public's affection and he was to win more major commissions. This stained-glass window was one of 15 designed for the Old Blandford Church in Petersburgh, Virginia. They were erected by the Southern States as a memorial to the Confederate dead of the Civil War.

IN · MEMORY · OF · THE · BRAVE · TEXANS · WHO
FELL · IN · AND · AROVND · PETERSBVRG · VIRGINIA
FOR · THE · CAVSE · THEY · KNEW · TO · BE · RIGHT
COME · FROM · THE · FOVR · WINDS · O · BREATH · AND ·
BREATHE · VPON · THESE · SLAIN · THAT · THEY · MAY · LIVE

TIFFANY STVDIOS
NEW YORK

CHAPTER NINE

RETURN TO GLORY

A Cypriot vase.

•

*The Louis C Tiffany
Foundation was
created as a centre for
American students of
arts and crafts. They
had access to
Tiffany's own art
collection and were
encouraged to
develop their own
talents. A student
group is pictured
dining at Laurelton
Hall.*

Louis Tiffany approached his seventies with the sad realization that the American art world was ignoring him. His work was no longer exhibited at the major art shows; he was perceived as an anachronism, a famous old man who lived in opulent splendour. The press interviewed him for his opinion on politics, and the popular magazines photographed his fantasy home. The serious art periodicals no longer wrote about his work.

Tiffany gave his lavish theatrical parties because he was anxious to convince society of his own artistic importance, and perhaps to counteract the ugliness, as he saw it, of contemporary art with demonstrations of beauty. Fabulous parties, with enormous quantities of food and drink, seem a less than serious attempt to preach this message.

The second educational party staged by Tiffany was a dinner for 150 men, who were asked to 'view the spring flowers'. A train was hired to transport them to Laurelton Hall. The gentlemen were served peacock, and the roasted birds brought to the tables by young ladies in Grecian costume.

On his birthday in 1916 he gave an extravagant champagne breakfast for hundreds of guests. They were entertained with a pageant, *The Quest for Beauty.*

It was devised as a sort of symphonic poem, and was acted by an all-socialite cast of 45. There was Beauty and Fire, and Painting, Music, Sculpture and Architecture. A proper stage was set up, and Louis spent $15,000 on the lighting effects alone.

These parties were bizarre, lavish and generous. In organizing them, in controlling and directing set-designs, costumes, lighting and music, Tiffany must have experienced the old excitement of a studio bustling with creative activity. But Louis gave his parties up for another altogether grander project. Although S Bing had died in 1905, and Louis had lost his intimate contact with the European artistic world, he remembered the work Van de Velde had done at the Weimar Kunstgewerbeschule. This was now an important school of design, and Walter Gropius, who became principal in 1919, was to make it internationally famous. Tiffany wanted Laurelton Hall to become an important art school in the United States.

Tiffany the artist-artisan never had any formal training. He studied painting but his skilful craftsmanship, his profound technical knowledge of glass, lighting, ceramics, metalwork and dyeing were all self-taught. His sense of colour was innate, instinctive. His childhood was lived among beautiful things. It is not surpris-

●

LEFT The Tiffany Studios at Madison Avenue on 45th Street were sold in 1918, shortly after the inauguration of the Louis C Tiffany Foundation.

RIGHT Sarah Hanley,
who nursed Tiffany
through an illness in
his sixties, remained a
constant companion
until his death in
1933.

ing that he believed in the process of osmosis as applied to the appreciation of art and the development of creative skills. In 1918, he formed the Louis C Tiffany Foundation. He asked, among others, his son Charles to serve on the board. The minutes of the first meeting reveal considerable reserve on the part of various board members. 'Mr Tiffany's plan . . . is an old one. It antedates the present war and the new conditions which the war has brought about. He is putting that plan into action at a time when the future is filled with uncertainties.'

The school was housed in buildings separate from Laurelton Hall, but the students had access to the main house. Tiffany donated part of his collection to the Foundation, and a trust was set up to fund the scheme. Students were chosen for their proven ability, and had to be Americans aged between 25 and 35 years old. The first young artists and craftsmen arrived at Laurelton Hall in 1920. Apparently the only formal demand made of them was that they should mount an 'exhibition' each week, when Tiffany would arrive to view their work. Otherwise, they were left to observe the artefacts of many cultures, and to motivate themselves into creative action.

Louis Tiffany sold the building that housed the Tiffany Studios at 345 Madison Avenue when he started the Louis C Tiffany Foundation. The Studios fell into a steady, slow decline, which is perhaps what the members of the Board feared. The last major commission undertaken by Tiffany Studios was the decoration of

the Presidential Palace in Havana, Cuba, in 1917. In 1932, Tiffany Studios petitioned for bankruptcy. When Joseph Briggs died in 1938, the Studios finally closed. The Foundation was forced to sell Laurelton Hall in 1946, as the upkeep of the mansion was so expensive. There is no art school to carry Louis Tiffany's name into posterity, although the Foundation continues to sponsor art students.

Tiffany retreated into his own private world. He was, of course, the same energetic, egocentric and creative person he had always been, ill at ease with small talk and light conversation. But, previously, he had been an important artist, extremely hardworking, and this social awkwardness had not been a handicap. Now, as a shy old man, he was seen as eccentric and odd. His constant companion was a young Irish woman, Sarah Hanley. Louis met her when she came to nurse him for a minor kidney ailment he suffered in his sixties. He persuaded her to stay with him, and she lived with him until he died. Sarah Hanley perfectly exemplifies the Tiffany osmosis effect. He met her when she was a nurse, and she came from a simple background. Under his tuition, she became a painter of some repute. She called Tiffany 'Padre' and always wore yellow, his favourite colour. Together, they painted and sketched the gardens and plants in Laurelton Hall. They painted studies of each other and went on painting trips to Florida. Louis built her a house on the Laurelton Hall estate, and decorated it with specially designed furniture and with artefacts from his collection. Sarah Hanley lived there until her death in 1958. Louis Comfort Tiffany died on 17 January 1933 at his 72nd Street home, and his work was neglected for many years afterward.

Aesthetic values changed with new technology. The Weimar Kunstgewerbeschule had been transformed into the Bauhaus, and this school designed furniture and buildings of a severe functionalism from plastic, steel and concrete, the new materials of mass-production. The undulating lines of Art Nouveau were perceived as grotesque, and the movement lacked any philosophical basis to sustain itself. Art Nouveau artists had pandered to a parvenu excitement in lavish display and, in the giddiness of this market, their work had become an orgy of ornamental decoration. Unchecked by any virile convictions, their convoluted line spiralled inward in narcissistic self-expression. This decadence of Art Nouveau was at variance with the powerful egalitarian and socialist philosophies that emerged after the First World War.

Louis Comfort Tiffany was a child – and father – of Art Nouveau. All his life, he was surrounded by wealth and luxury; he could indulge in any and all of his inter-

LEFT *Paperweight, or 'reactive', glass was the product of a complicated process. These vases were made by this technique. Height (from left to right) 5 in (13 cm), 17 in (43.5 cm), 9 in (23 cm).*

RIGHT Tiffany visited many archaeological sites around the Mediterranean. He designed these 'Samian' vases in homage to the craft of ancient Samos. Height (from left to right) 3 in (8 cm), 15 in (38.5 cm).

FAR RIGHT Tiffany collected American Indian artefacts. Their influence is seen in the design of this hanging lamp.

ests. Even in his lifetime, people were awed and likened him to a Medici prince, so extravagant were his talents and his manner of living. Other Art Nouveau artists had similarly wealthy backgrounds – James McNeill Whistler, for example, was the son of a railroad magnate.

The Favrile glass objects created by Louis Tiffany were thrown away, his interiors were demolished, and his great stained-glass windows and mosaics now considered fussy and overpowering were smashed up. Louis Tiffany had been convinced that, even if the art critics rejected him, the great American Public would not. Once more, in his vanity, he underestimated his true value. There is no denying his prodigious output, his extraordinary skill and talent, and that, for two decades, he stamped his aesthetic values on the domestic style of the United States. But this is not his major achievement.

RIGHT This delicate
vase recalls the long-
stemmed perfume
bottles of Persia.
Height 11 in (28 cm).

LEFT Since his days as a young painter, Tiffany was recognized as a great colourist. It was his ability to translate this talent in glass that brought him lasting fame. Height (from left to right) 6 in (15 cm), 7 in (18 cm), 9 in (23 cm).

T I F F A N Y

•

RIGHT An iridescent Millefiori vase of organic design and vibrant blues and greens so typical of Art Nouveau. Height 7 in (18 cm).

FAR RIGHT A glass urn made of iridescent Favrile. Height 26 in (66 cm).

BELOW RIGHT Gold curves, reminiscent of Islamic calligraphy, pattern a muted dark-blue surface.

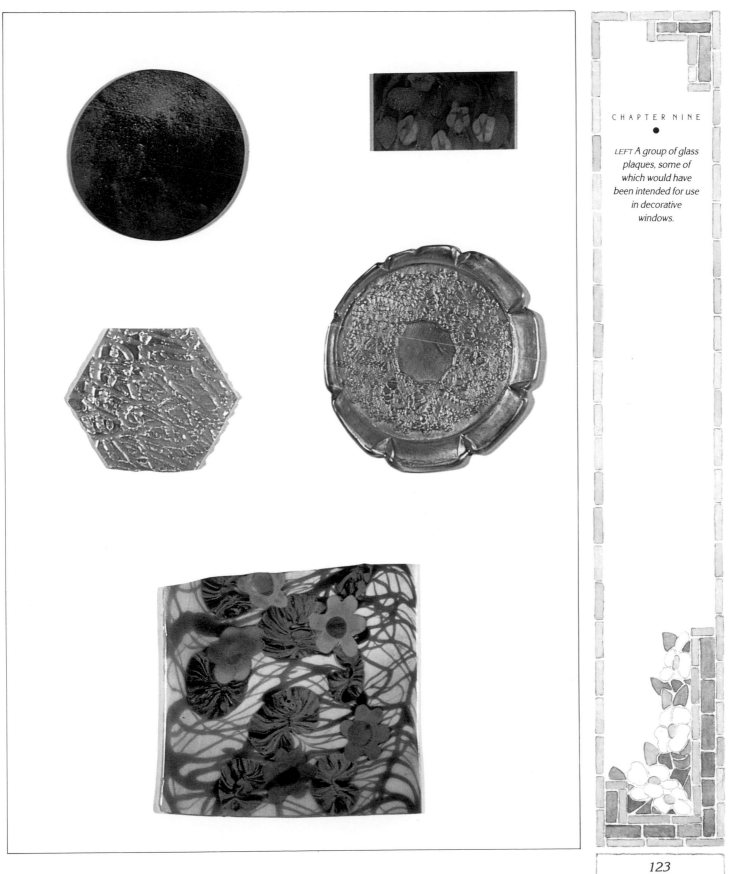

LEFT A group of glass plaques, some of which would have been intended for use in decorative windows.

CONCLUSION

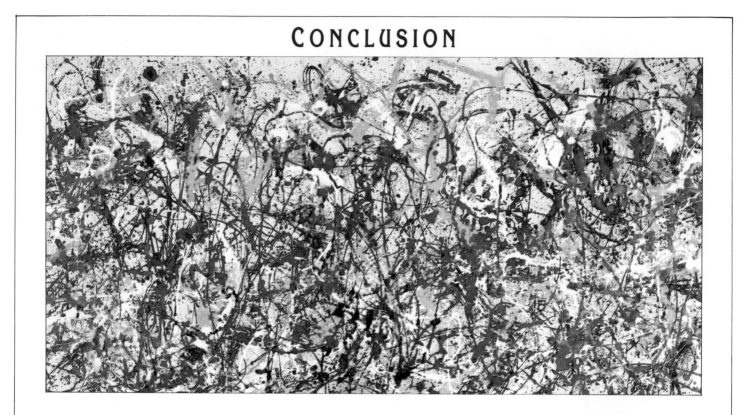

TOP Jackson Pollack's painting Autumn Rhythm *established the American art movement known as Abstract Expressionism.*

ABOVE AND RIGHT
Tiffany's Favrile vases expressed an almost abstract freedom of design in their form and colour.

The true genius of Tiffany lies in the spontaneous and free-flowing forms of his glass objects. In these, and in his stained-glass paintings, the natural properties of the material are used to create the image. Louis C Tiffany is seen as a precursor of Abstract Expressionism, a specifically American art movement, the leaders of which were Jackson Pollock and Robert Motherwell. In the 1950s, this school rescued Favrile glass from obscurity and derision. The glass objects were acknowledged as the earliest examples of pure form and colour expressed through free design. Tiffany had allowed his medium to express emotion without representation, and for this his genius is recognized.

Tiffany cut the umbilical cord that bound American art to Europe. He rejected the traditions of the Old World. He looked to nature and to the Orient, and, in expressing his emotions through colour and form, Tiffany prompted the development of an American aesthetic.

His work continues to divide critical opinion, but he is no longer neglected. In the perverse way of the art world, a prodigious output is regarded with some suspicion. A few words originally used to describe Favrile glass make a fitting epitaph for Louis Comfort Tiffany: an individual who was 'bizarre and extravagant, but always convincing and of great taste and distinction'.

FOOTNOTES AND BIBLIOGRAPHY

FOOTNOTES

INTRODUCTION

1. Albert Christian Revi, *American Art Nouveau Glass*, Thomas Nelson & Sons, New York, 1968.
2. Robert Schmutzler, *Art Nouveau*, Thames & Hudson, London, 1978.
3. S. Bing, *Artistic America, Tiffany Glass and Art Nouveau*, Massachusetts Institute of Technology Press, Cambridge, Mass., 1970.

CHAPTER ONE: EAST-WEST ENCOUNTERS

1. Gertrude Speenburgh, *The Arts of the Tiffanys*, Lightner Publishing Corp., Illinois, 1956.
2. *Dictionary of Art and Artists*, edited by Peter and Linda Murray, Penguin, London, 1959.
3. Robert Koch, *Louis C Tiffany: Rebel in Glass,* Crown Publishers Inc., New York, 1964.
4. Ibid.

CHAPTER TWO: A RICH USE OF PAINT

1. S. Bing, *Artistic America, Tiffany Glass and Art Nouveau,* **see above.**
2. Gertrude Speenburgh, *The Arts of the Tiffanys,* **see above.**
3. *Dictionary of Art and Artists*, edited by Peter and Linda Murray, **see above.**
4. Gertrude Speenburgh, **see above.**
5. Candace Wheeler, *The Development of Embroidery in America*, Harper & Brothers, New York, 1921.

CHAPTER FIVE: PAINTINGS IN GLASS

1. S. Bing, *Artistic America, Tiffany Glass and Art Nouveau,* **see above.**
2. Ibid.

All quotes from Louis Comfort Tiffany are taken from his lectures and the book *The Artwork of Louis C. Tiffany,* by Charles de Kay, published by Doubleday, Page & Co., New York, 1914.

BIBLIOGRAPHY

Amaya, Mario, *Tiffany Glass*, Walker & Co., New York, 1976.

Bailey, Stephen and Garner, Phillipe, *Twentieth-Century Style and Design*, Thames & Hudson, London, 1986.

Baur, John I. H., *Revolution and Tradition in Modern American Art*, Harvard University Press, Cambridge, 1951.

Bing, S., *Artistic America, Tiffany Glass and Art Nouveau*, Massachusetts Institute of Technology Press, Cambridge, Mass., 1970

Doros, Paul E., *The Tiffany Collection of the Chrysler Museum at Norfolk*, Chrysler Museum, Norfolk, Va., 1978.

Duncan, Alistair, *Light and Landscape in Tiffany Windows*, Simon & Schuster, New York, 1980.

Garner, Phillipe (Ed.), *Phaidon Encyclopedia of Decorative Arts*, Phaidon Press Ltd., Oxford, 1979.

Heydt, G. F., *Charles L. Tiffany and the House of Tiffany & Co.*, Tiffany & Co., New York, 1893.

Koch, Robert, *Louis Comfort Tiffany: Rebel in Glass*, Crown Publishers Inc., New York, 1982.

Lambourne, Lionel, *Utopian Graftsmen*, Peregrine Smith Inc., Salt Lake City, 1980.

Leish, Kenneth W., *White House*, Newsweek, New York, 1972.

Revi, Albert Christian, *American Art Nouveau Glass*, Thomas Nelson & Sons, New York, 1968.

Schmutzler, Robert, *Art Nouveau*, Thames & Hudson, London, 1978.

Speenburgh, Gertrude, *The Arts of the Tiffanys*, Lightner Publishing Corp., Illinois, 1956.

Watkinson, Ray, *William Morris as Designer*, Trefoil Books Ltd., London, 1981.

CONCLUSION

INDEX

TIFFANY

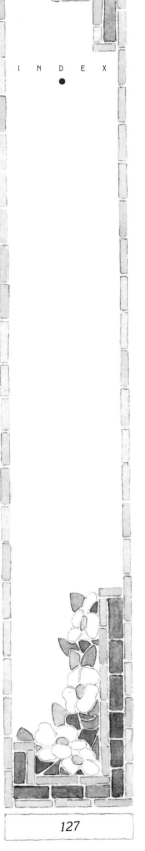

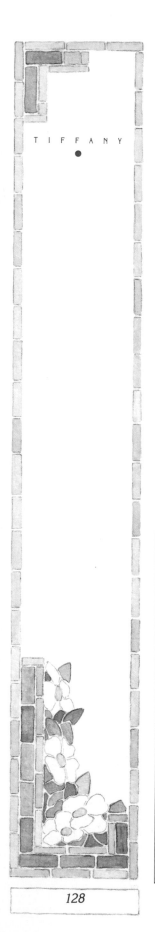

PICTURE CREDITS

Key: *t* = top; *b* = bottom; *l* = left; *r* = right; *f* = far.

The author and publishers have made every effort to identify the copyright owners of the pictures used in this publication; they apologize for any omissions and would like to thank the following: